Acclaim for *MindShifting* ...

"Joshua Ehrlich has taken the complicated concept of mindfulness and simplified it for busy executives. His ability to explain ideas clearly, and then offer ways to reflect and process them, makes this an easy to read and easy to apply book. His authentic and personal approach to storytelling brings his ideas to life."
— **Jose Davila,** Vice President, Corporate Human Resources, GAP, Inc.

"Josh Ehrlich's *MindShifting* offers a panoply of ideas to improve one's effectiveness, whether it is personal or professional. Anyone who picks up this book cannot help but find several approaches that will resonate with them. I have seen Josh's recommendations on the importance of sleep and the creation of your own personal board of directors presented as development initiatives for leaders in organizations in which I worked. When implemented, both drove leader effectiveness as well as improved quality of thought and decision making."
— **Liz Dunlap,** SVP & Chief People Officer, Panera Bread

"*MindShifting* provides invaluable insight, tools, and resources to address the central issues of our age. How do leaders show up effectively with all the demands on their time and attention? And how do they chart a clear course with the information overload, ambiguity, and speed of modern business? This book shows the way."
— **Diane Hessan,** CEO, Communispace

"*MindShifting* transforms thinking to produce better outcomes. It encourages the reader to think about how we think. It includes practical 'experiments' to help the reader try new incremental approaches to learning and change. This intriguing 'how to' manual celebrates mindfulness. This book has the potential to be life altering. Every person interested in a more productive existence can benefit from *MindShifting*."
— **Rich Smith,** Vice President, Human Resources, at Kaiser Permanente

"Josh Ehrlich has made a major contribution in *MindShifting*. The book does a terrific job of drawing on research and theory to build an extremely pragmatic and useful way of thinking about leadership and learning. Numerous cases and examples, combined with very effective tips and tools make this a valuable guide for leaders. *MindShifting* provides a terrific roadmap for improving your leadership effectiveness in the context of the tremendously demanding environment of today's world."
— **David A. Nadler,** Vice Chairman, Marsh & McLennan Companies
and author of *Champions of Change, Organizational Architecture
and Building Better Boards*

"As we all strive to get more done faster, we actually achieve less. In this breakthrough book, Josh uses the full depth of his experience and expertise to show us how to look at the world from the inside out. His focus is more on who we are rather than what we do. More importantly, Josh describes a number of simple, easy to use tools and techniques that everyone can use immediately to become a better leader."
— **Paul J. Gallagher,** Managing Director, TIAA-CREF

MindShifting

FOCUS FOR PERFORMANCE

Joshua Ehrlich

PORTAL
BOOKS

2011
Portal Books
An imprint of SteinerBooks / Anthroposophic Press, Inc.
610 Main Street, Great Barrington, MA 01230
www.steinerbooks.org

Copyright © 2012 by Joshua Ehrlich
Cover design: Stefan Killen / stefankillendesign.com
Book design: John Eagleson / johneagleson.com

Library of Congress Cataloging-in-Publication Data

Ehrlich, Joshua.
    Mindshifting : focus for performance / Joshua Ehrlich.
      p.   cm.
    Includes bibliographical references.
    ISBN 978-0-9831984-3-7
    1. Executive coaching. 2. Leadership.   I. Title.
  HD30.4.E397 2012
  658.4'07124 – dc23   2011048319

ISBN 978-0-9831984-4-4 (eBook)

Contents

Part III
Overcoming Five Destructive Habits

Part IV
Conclusions and Implications

Foreword

I first met Josh Ehrlich in 2005 when he coached me as part of J. P. Morgan's Leadership and Development Program. It was a transformational experience. He prepared me to face the challenges of a newly minted managing director working for a large global Wall Street bank.

His coaching helped me realize the importance of learning from the within. It allowed me to build upon who I was and to realize my unique strengths. I learned techniques that enabled me to address challenges and accomplish goals. In doing so I learned to challenge myself, avoid limiting assumptions, and experiment with taking calculated risks. I started to explore ways of creating innovative solutions and so deliver business results. In short, Josh focused me on what I needed to do not just as a manager but as a leader. His coaching and these skills proved critical to my professional success in the years that followed.

Switching companies, I relocated to London in May 2008 to run Lehman Brothers' European Middle East and Africa Operations. Immediately I was faced with a myriad of challenges that would ultimately test my leadership skills: Against the background of the credit crisis, I needed to establish myself quickly in my new position. That involved winning acceptance in a tightly knit relationship-driven environment and adapting to the new organizational culture. Five months into the job I was leading a team of more than five hundred professionals during the dark and stressful days of the demise and eventual bankruptcy of Lehman Brothers, through to its eventual part acquisition by the Japanese investment bank Nomura. That I successfully made that transition was a tribute to Josh's teaching and techniques.

The challenges I faced at Nomura brought home to me every aspect of leadership. It required integrating two sets of employees, changing the business model, and building a scalable global platform from a regional one. All of this, while bringing together the best of Eastern and Western cultures with all the intricacies that that involved. My time with Josh and what I had built upon over the preceding three years held me in strong stead.

For executives leading their organizations through change and growth, *MindShifting* provides a powerful tool kit. The book guides you through the seven attentional shifts a leader has to make, providing a logical framework for you to move from managing one's self to leading large organizations. Throughout the thought-provoking chapters, you move from doing to leading, from exchanging information to communicating, from relationship building to networking, from self-development to team building, from personal accountability to organizational authority, from task analysis to market analysis, and from self-awareness to interpersonal awareness.

MindShifting is well structured and easy to read and implement. The core concepts and techniques are introduced and built upon gradually. Utilizing real case studies, the book guides you from theory to practicality, providing valuable and practical insights to everyday challenges. *MindShifting* also serves as a self-assessment tool allowing you to create a personal development plan as well as structural goal-setting for your organization. By focusing on the real-life skills an executive needs in today's world, this book leads you on a journey to reach your full potential.

Reading *MindShifting* has proven invaluable for me. Not only has it been a great opportunity to refresh and reflect on the skills Josh coached me on, but it has added new dimensions to my thought process. I am now aware of *MindShifting* as a powerful and effective approach to successful leadership development.

I sincerely hope that others find it as useful as I have.

Garth Barker-Goldie
Senior Managing Director
Global Head of Wholesale Operations
Nomura International plc

Chapter 1

The Challenge

Here is how a senior executive described her day:

> I just returned from vacation (which felt more like a flexible work arrangement given how often I looked at my handheld) and have already been on seven calls/meetings today beginning at 7:30 a.m., did email in between (and some during), ran to the airport, edited two presentation decks, took a call before the first flight, left three voicemails, read an article about best practices while I ate bad Mexican food, took another call, typed while walking on the moving sidewalk, about to board the next flight and still have to prep tonight for my 7:00 a.m. meeting tomorrow.

If this sounds familiar you are in good company. At home and at work we never stop. Everyone around us is also racing, so we naturally fall in step with their accelerating rhythm.[1] If we are honest, we know that being so busy makes us restless, scattered, and distracted. We need to be able to focus our attention and step back from the action to make better decisions and to learn.

We live in an age that requires us to manage information, and there is a flood of it coming from all sides. With personal and handheld computers, we can choose when, how, and where we work. But we have less control of when, how, and where we can think without interruption. The same technology that enables us to be more productive also undermines our focus. To manage information we need to manage ourselves, and this means managing our attention.

Consider that as professionals we consume three times the quantity of information that we did in 1960.[2] This means watching more television as well as:

- Checking email 50 times a day

- Sending/receiving 178 texts or emails

- Checking 40 different websites

- Changing programs/windows 37 times an hour

It is amazing that we have adapted to handle this volume at all. Computer scientists describe this "human-computer system" almost as a new life form.[3] We have evolved and invented machines to serve our needs that are no longer separate from us. If we step back from this science fiction matrix, we see how dramatically we underestimate the impact of this technology. A study by the technology research firm Basex estimated information overload and fractured attention costs the U.S. economy $900 billion a year.[4]

Then there is the physical, emotional, and interpersonal toll that we are just starting to appreciate. A significant portion of our experience is now fragmented, and so our consciousness becomes fragmented. This challenges our ability to build relationships and maintain empathic connections. When I am absorbed in my computer screen I don't notice my wife or daughter playing across the room. If I don't pay attention, I can't engage, and I can't show I care. If an essential part of being human is connecting and showing caring, then my addiction to the buzz of technology is a fundamental threat.

Continual multitasking seems to be a necessity to keep up with technology and society. Unfortunately imaging studies suggest that our brains cannot perform two cognitive tasks at once. What we are actually doing is switching rapidly between them. The more tasks, the less attention we give to each and the more time we lose switching back and forth. Studies show our performance consistently goes down when we take on many things at once. However, we consistently overrate how well we will do.[5] The brain is not very good at multitasking, but it is very good at deluding itself.

Multitasking may be needed in some individual contributor roles that require quick and efficient transactions. If you are a bus driver, waiter, or trader on the floor of an exchange, you need to continually be watching for new information while solving problems, and simultaneously executing a number of tasks. If you are a professional or leader, though, you need to think ahead, solve complex problems and monitor progress toward goals. This requires disciplined focus and active, sustained concentration.

My clients seek help because they find themselves stuck in a variety of ways. They typically respond by trying to work faster and harder — essentially doing more of the same. Unfortunately this strategy just leaves them worn out. Running their engines at top speed, there are too many things flying by for them to be able to attend to and take in anything new. By taking their foot off the gas, they can learn different strategies and actually get where they are going faster.

Wendy worked her way up from an assistant to a successful senior executive by learning to shift her attention. She was able to let go of what initially made her effective (getting things done on her own) in order to focus on what she needed to do as a leader (developing her team and facilitating their work). Simon was a skeptical fifty-nine-year-old operations executive who spent thirty years methodically solving problems and checking them off his list. He learned to challenge his self-limiting assumptions, experiment with taking calculated risks, and create an innovative vision. Rod was a former Russian tank commander who ruled with intellect and intimidation. Emotionally tone deaf and caring for little besides his own agenda, he had a great deal of trouble influencing. Rod learned to listen and tune in to feelings, thus inviting rather than demanding his colleagues' attention.

My clients' success stories are woven through each chapter. These are fantastic and talented leaders who work in a range of Fortune 500 and smaller companies including Pfizer, Diageo, Deutsche Bank, UBS, BCBS, Misys, New York Life, Pitney Bowes, and Merrill Lynch. I have used pseudonyms and changed biographical details unless clients specifically asked me to include their story. Their examples can help inspire you to make difficult changes and unlock your potential.

My academic and research training is as a clinical psychologist. My work and passion is coaching people to lead their organizations and manage their careers. In addition to working with senior executives and their teams, I teach leadership programs and supervise and accredit coaches. This book summarizes the principles I teach my students and clients. It is a personal guide for you to learn and manage your development. My clients and I have personally tested everything I recommend. In addition, my conclusions are backed by established research in the social, biological, and behavioral sciences.

I will teach you a new way to think and accomplish your goals. To succeed you first need to **stop the action** and clear the noise in your head. Then **reflection** enables you to observe what you are doing and modify your approach. Learning to **focus and manage your attention** is like adjusting a spotlight. It enables you to see more clearly where you are going and what could get in your way. Figuring out where to focus is not just about prioritization. It is about paying attention to landmarks and clues on the road that can help you learn. This book will guide you in how and where to focus in order to learn essential leadership and professional skills.

Many books describe exemplary leadership and provide lists of behaviors to practice. Meta-reviews describe how this "outside in" approach can be problematic in how we study and develop leaders.[6] We typically measure the effectiveness of leaders by collecting information about how well leaders are regarded by their colleagues. In 360° surveys we sum up ratings in all directions — from peers, direct reports, and clients. While this information is relevant to the environment leaders create around them, ratings of perceived effectiveness are highly influenced by our feelings toward the leaders (i.e., how well we like them). These measures resemble political polling numbers in an election.

Leadership development programs take 360° data and try to get leaders to learn and demonstrate behaviors that will lead to higher ratings. The problem is that leading from the outside in this way only takes you so far. Helping leaders look good and be approved of advances their careers, but does not necessarily drive the performance of organizations. A study of the British military in the nineteenth and twentieth centuries showed that officers concerned with status and promotion caused the deaths of thousands of soldiers. These officers got promoted by managing impressions more than demonstrating skills at leading.[7] Studies of Fortune 500 companies similarly find that CEO charisma predicts how much they are paid, but not how well they perform.[8] Boards of directors seem to overvalue how good a CEO looks on the outside.

Applying the disciplines of reflection and attention is learning and leading from the *inside out*. The *inside out* approach leverages your inner compass — your feelings, intuitions, and values. Building on who you are and your unique strengths is at the heart of effective and authentic leadership.[9] Once you develop your signature leadership style, picking up on subtle clues around and inside you make it possible to adjust your approach on the fly. Daniel Goleman studied a range of leadership styles and found that leaders who coach and delegate authority are more effective than coercive leaders.[10] However, he found that the most effective leaders used their emotional intelligence to read the environment and flex their leadership style in the moment.

My experience coaching from the inside out is also consistent with studies of value-centered leaders. Leaders who are motivated by core values and purpose have greater and more sustainable impact on their organizations.[11] Jim Collins investigated Fortune 1000 companies that went from performing below average to above average over a thirty-year period.[12] The eleven companies that fit this profile each improved after a new CEO took over. These CEOs had three things in common — they were modest, humble and persistent.

An extensive review of leadership behavior and best practices in a range of industries reached a similar conclusion that runs counter to our stereotype of the tough, hard-nosed CEO.[13] The most effective senior leaders demonstrated a single remarkable characteristic: kindness. Charismatic, heavy-handed CEOs may transform their personal wealth, but kind, self-effacing, and inner-directed CEOs transform their organizations.

Kindness does not mean "soft" management. There is ample evidence that extraordinary results can be achieved by setting clear, unequivocal, and high expectations of employees and then sticking to them.[14] This may sound harsh, but is not about being coercive or domineering. "Demanding" performance improvement can actually be extremely empowering when employees are called to step up and allowed to rise to the challenge.

Learning from the *inside out* has traditionally meant generating insights from psychotherapy to make the unconscious more conscious. Here I am adding the idea of focusing our attention and getting curious about specific internal and external cues in order to become more aware. You can use the inside out approach to increase your empathy, for example, which is the basis of emotional intelligence and invaluable for building relationships and leading. Start by focusing on physical clues in your body. Learn to trust the uncomfortable tension in your stomach as anxiety, and read the flush in your face as anger. Then pay attention to nonverbal signals in others so you can determine what they are feeling. Connecting your feelings with their impact on others is the basis of empathy.

Many of the key concepts I discuss are exemplified in experiments in each chapter. As these are essential to understanding and absorbing the principles, I recommend at least reading through them. However, do not feel you have to try every experiment. Read until you find one that resonates with you, then stop and give yourself time to work with it before moving on. This will help you put your learning into action without overloading you with activities. Don't take my word for these ideas. Get curious and experiment for yourself.

There are four parts of this book:

I. **Three Core Disciplines and Their Application to Learning** develops the foundation of stopping, reflecting, and focusing. These are then applied to learning. You will use these skills throughout the rest of the book, so take your time here.

II. **A Map, a Compass, and Seven Essential Skills** introduces "Mind-Shifts." These are a set of seven attentional shifts you need to make as you learn to lead. Assessing yourself using the MindShifts map will help you create an initial plan for your development. Values and purpose form the inner compass that guides you. I then show you where to focus to learn the seven essential skills, each of which builds on the others. Strategic and innovative thinking are two sides of a coin. Communication helps you build relationships, and managing stress helps you be more emotionally intelligent. Together these skills enable you to lead and develop teams.

III. **Overcoming Five Destructive Habits** helps you understand the nature of habits and a variety of ways to undo them. We fall into habits in how we think, treat ourselves, manage uncertainty, interact and engage with technology. These habits interfere with your learning, applying leadership skills, and achieving your objectives. Learning strategies to shake off habits can help you when you feel yourself start to struggle and go off track.

IV. **Conclusions and Implications** helps you complete your development plan and then applies goal-setting to organizations. The final chapter goes beyond questions of effectiveness to ask larger questions of purpose and the nature of attention. These questions are especially important as we think about the leadership we need in the future and a vision for the next generation of leaders.

Michelle Obama expressed concern to Valerie Jarrett, a senior White House advisor, that the president's schedule did not give him time to think. Of all the important issues the president needs to make time for, what he needs most is the ability to reflect and focus. All successful leaders must find the time and carve it out, and once they have it, they need to know how to use it. This applies equally well to all of us as we lead and navigate our lives.

Part I

Three Core Disciplines and Their Application to Learning

Overview

The first thing to do is to stop doing. Thinking, creating, and leading are impossible when you are scrambling to keep up with your never-ending To-Do list. However, it is hard to stop when everyone around you is running at top speed. So stopping, which sounds simple, actually requires significant self-discipline and practice.

Once you have learned to stop for a moment you can look objectively at yourself. You can decide whether you are headed in the right direction and how well you are doing getting there. Focusing your attention enables you to see more clearly and to pick out clues inside and around you. This helps you make better decisions.

When you can stop, reflect, and focus, you can learn. The principles of natural selection apply to leaders too. It is not the strongest or smartest that succeed; it is those who can adapt most readily. Learning and adapting can be enhanced with focus and attention. Leadership skills are complex and difficult to acquire, but you can learn how to learn in order to develop these skills.

Spiritual traditions have been developing the mental disciplines of reflection and focus for centuries. Techniques for learning concentration and contemplation are central to the mystical teachings of Christianity, Judaism, Hinduism, Shamanism, and Islam. Buddhism describes **mindfulness** as both a state of mind and an attitude. The state of mind is

present-focused awareness, open-mindedness, and acceptance. It takes great practice and willpower to live in the present, rather than ruminating about the past or worrying about the future. In addition, staying open to new ideas can bring up significant anxiety, and accepting reality can challenge our sense of identity. It helps a great deal to cultivate a **welcoming, curious, and gentle attitude** toward ourselves and our experience. It is the combination of state of mind and attitude that makes mindfulness invaluable.

Mindfulness is based on three useful components: selective attention (focusing where we want), sustained attention (focusing as long as we want), and attention switching (changing focus when we want).[1] Mindfulness helps reduce stress, in part by increasing your ability to pick up physical clues. These clues tell you what you are feeling and what you need to take care of yourself. Mindfulness also increases empathy and the ability to read social cues including others' emotions.[2] Thus it facilitates your ability to self-monitor through greater access to feedback.[3]

Research demonstrates mindfulness training has a wide range of additional benefits:[4] Mindfulness training enhances positive emotions and emotional stability. In addition, mindfulness increases immunological functioning and reduces depression and chronic pain. When we can accept reality as it is, we become less frustrated by our situation, less fearful of change, and less depressed about not achieving our fantasies.

We are just starting to appreciate the power that reflection and mindfulness have to facilitate learning. In an elegant series of studies, Ellen Langer at Harvard found that individuals who apply reflection and mindfulness are able to learn more quickly, problem solve more creatively, and extrapolate their learning more flexibly across settings.[5] The more we can tolerate anxiety and discomfort, the more we can take the personal risks we need to learn.

Langer demonstrated another dramatic impact of mindfulness. She offered mindfulness training to a group of nursing home patients and compared them to a group who did not receive the training. The mindfulness group lived significantly longer. Perhaps this was because of the direct impact of mindfulness on immunological responsiveness. Or perhaps reopening their senses and savoring experience gave the patients more reason to live.

Experiment: Mindful Breathing and Biofeedback

How do you know when you are on the edge and running on empty? A proven approach is to hook up biofeedback monitors to measure dimensions such as your heart rate, respiration and blood pressure. Watching the monitors gives you feedback that helps you tune in to your physiological reactions and control them. This helps you relax and reduces your stress along with its negative consequences.[6]

Your breathing is a built-in stress barometer and focusing tool that enables you to get the same results without external monitors. When you are tense, your breathing is typically shallow and fast. When you are relaxed, your breathing is deeper and more regular. Simply paying attention to how you are breathing can reset its natural rhythm and enable you to ratchet down. Building a closer connection with your breath is an invaluable first step as you learn to stop and focus.

• Take a minute and watch your breathing. Notice your stomach rising and falling as you follow your breath all the way in and all the way out. See if your breathing slows and your muscles relax without any added effort.

• It can be helpful to say "In" and "Out" to yourself as you breathe. After a couple of cycles add, "Deep" and "Slow" to your in breath and your out breath. You are not trying to breathe deeper or slower, just saying these words to yourself. See if they help you focus and if they alter breathing.

• You may notice that after doing this exercise for a few minutes your mind begins to clear. You may also feel your thoughts getting more urgent and racing faster. Your mind will naturally do this sometimes, and it can take some time for the noise to quiet down. Think of a glass of freshly squeezed juice. If you let it sit, gradually the pulp will settle to the bottom and the top will become clear. But this takes time, and happens only if we let go and wait. We cannot force it. We need to allow it to happen on its own.

Becoming more able to stop, reflect, and focus is a tremendous challenge. Exercises like mindful breathing are not hard to do, but integrating them into your daily routine and mastering them takes ongoing determination. It takes considerable commitment to regularly pull out of the action and allow your swirl to settle, especially as technology and the increasing pace of society keep working to stir you up. Reflection and focus are powerful allies that help you become more effective and learn core leadership skills. However, you need to be patient with yourself and manage your expectations in order to reap their benefits. You will also need to find regular reminders to make these practices a habit and part of the way you live.

◆ ◆ ◆

Chapter 2

Stopping

Albert Einstein liked to go out and sail for hours. He would lean back and let the wind take him, often coming to rest on a sandy island. There he sat until friends or family came to fetch him. He wasn't goofing off. Sailing allowed him to relax, eliminate distractions, and focus on his job — **thinking.** You might argue that while taking time to go sailing sounds great, you are not a theoretical physicist and your work requires you to stay in an office. But if I asked your boss, I bet she would say you were hired for your ability to think, not your ability to do. And if you are like most people, you spend a lot more time doing than thinking. **Your first foundation then is making time to stop the action and think.**

As the chief strategist of a large technology firm, Steve had huge demands on his time and attention. He felt he could never stop and spent almost no time dedicated to thinking. Rather, like many senior executives, his time was spent interacting or transacting. His conversations in meetings with colleagues offered him useful insights, but this was not a substitute for thinking time on his own. This was especially ironic and frustrating for him because his job as chief strategist was to think ahead and create new products, which he had no time to do. His solution was to block out two-hour periods three times each week to stop and think. Over the course of a couple of months he generated several groundbreaking product ideas. He spearheaded the launch of two of these products, which produced significant new revenue streams for his firm. Steve now jealously guards his thinking time, given how invaluable it has become.

Steve's situation is quite common. The more responsibility we get in organizations, the less control we often have over our time. We have to be creative about making time to think, and part of the solution lies in asking for help:

- *Assistants.* If you have an assistant, or can get one, ask the assistant's help in saving space between meetings and making sure the appointments are prioritized. An assistant can also help you anticipate and clear time for you to prepare for important meetings. Many of my clients don't ask for this kind of help because they think they always need to be accessible and say yes to every request. But self-protection is not selfish. It is an essential prerequisite to serving others.

- *Delegation and team support.* Give away tasks that bog you down and let go of the belief that no one can do it as well as you. If you tend to be impatient, hire more reflective team members to complement you, and tell them not to be shy about challenging you. Get your team to push back on your decisions if they see you staying too involved in details.

- *Setting boundaries.* Be clear with colleagues about your needs and limits. If you can't meet a deadline or respond to a request quickly, say so. Similar conversations about your availability may help with your family, especially if you decide to sometimes work at home. Working at home can give you freedom from interruptions at the office, but it can also bring up other distractions if you are not careful.

Carving out time is the first step. But unless you can focus during your thinking time, it may not be that productive. Microsoft studied its employees to determine the cost of interruptions from email and instant messaging.[1] The irony is that they found many of their own products interfere with their employees' ability to finish tasks. Employees were interrupted on average four times an hour by email, and three times an hour by instant messages. Overall, 57 percent of tasks got interrupted. After each interruption it took employees between ten and fifteen minutes to get back to the original task. In 27 percent of cases it took employees more than two hours to get back to the original task! If you add face-to-face and phone interruptions, which they did not include in the study, it seems we spend more time getting interrupted and trying to refocus than working. No wonder Bill Gates used to spend two weeks a year in a secluded cabin in order to review his engineers' proposals for the future.

You can get better at managing interruptions by using the ACT method.[2] The idea is to think carefully about whether to accept, curtail, or triage interruptions:

- *Accept:* This is our default choice. Most of the time we just accept interruptions and handle the issue then and there. Employees in the Microsoft study reported feeling socially obligated to respond to email and instant messages right away because there was someone waiting on the other end.

- *Curtail:* We can curtail interruptions by setting boundaries and making ourselves unavailable. Reserve a conference room and turn off your Blackberry for example (or rent a cabin in the woods like Bill Gates). Seclusion is an excellent option that most of us don't use often enough.

- *Triage:* Here you assess the importance of the interruption "on the field" before accepting it. Triaging includes negotiating expectations with the person who is interrupting. Is their need really urgent? Can they wait until you are finished with what you are doing? Exactly when do they need a specific answer?

Like hamsters on a wheel, we can't seem to stop. We find it rewarding to continually react and move items off our plate, rather than critically assessing what we are doing and where we are going. **We have the irrational belief that if we are not always doing something we are wasting time.** We need to challenge these beliefs and retrain ourselves so we can see the benefits of *not doing*.

In addition to not doing, we need to learn the value of not thinking. Not thinking makes room for insight. When you stop thinking it allows you to clear out your clutter and replenish your mental energy. Putting aside your daily tasks and allowing yourself to daydream enables you to discover new ideas and see beyond what is in front of you. Vacations and sleep are the cornerstones. In later chapters I describe techniques such as meditation and self-hypnosis that provide further help turning your mind away from thinking.

Besides giving us rest and recuperation, vacations (from the Latin *vacare*, "to empty") are a time to put out our mind's garbage. This is why all of the major religions prescribe at least one day of rest per week. Organizations typically offer vacations grudgingly, but some academic institutions and consulting firms understand that vacations can help them create thought leaders. They offer six-month sabbaticals so employees can clear the decks. Most of us don't have this option, and so need to be creative in finding space for ourselves.

• Start small and think about stopping in place. You don't have to leave work to make time to think. Make sure to regularly get away from your desk and daily routine. Find a quiet place in the building or go for a short walk around the block. If there are no other options, go to the bathroom for a minute and wash your face. The warm water on your skin can be relaxing and help you reset.

• Vacations should not be limited to long weekends or weeks away. Think about how often you make time for creative and fun activities. Going to artistic or cultural events, attending a workshop about something you know nothing about, and even taking a short walk can be mini-vacations from thinking. Give yourself permission to plan one in the next month and notice the impact.

• Europeans can get six or more weeks vacation. The table shows the 2009 average number of days paid annual leave in a number of countries.[3] By contrast U.S. employees average two weeks, but it is wasted on many of us.[4] Management Recruiters International surveyed executives and found that over half were not planning to use their vacation time.[5] What is stopping you from scheduling a vacation?

• When you go on vacation, do you fill your time with constant activity? Do you need to check your office voice mail and email every day? Or can you communicate your inaccessibility to your colleagues and find ways to get backup coverage? As one of my clients commented, "If you can't completely disconnect for two weeks without things falling apart, then there is something seriously wrong with how your work and team are organized." This can be hard because letting go means confronting our need to be needed.

AVERAGE NUMBER OF DAYS PAID ANNUAL LEAVE, BY COUNTRY (2009)

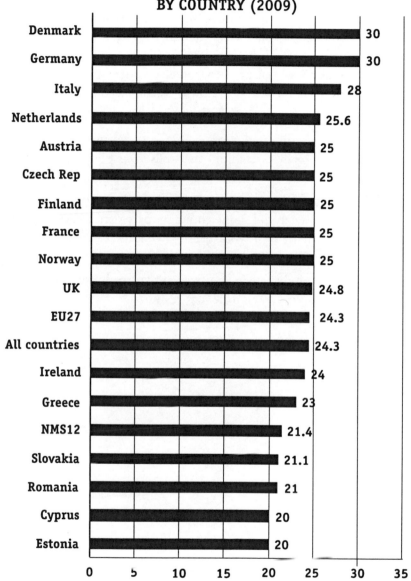

Country	Days
Denmark	30
Germany	30
Italy	28
Netherlands	25.6
Austria	25
Czech Rep	25
Finland	25
France	25
Norway	25
UK	24.8
EU27	24.3
All countries	24.3
Ireland	24
Greece	23
NMS12	21.4
Slovakia	21.1
Romania	21
Cyprus	20
Estonia	20

Experiment: Stopping to Sleep

Stopping regularly is part of our natural biological rhythm. If our minds don't turn off for seven to nine hours each day we go a little crazy. We get cranky, can't concentrate, have delayed reactions and have trouble remembering things.[6] Two out of every three of your colleagues are not getting enough sleep, but you can establish restful sleep by getting into good habits.[7]

• Go to bed and wake up at the same time, and set up a ritual (e.g., pajamas, brushing teeth, stretching) that tells your body that sleep is coming.

• Often we can't sleep because our minds are still whirring from the day. Write down any troublesome thoughts or worries before going to bed. This gets them out of your head so you don't have to actively think about them now.

• If you are having trouble sleeping and want to read more, Schwartz and Aaron's *Somniquest* is an excellent resource.[8]

◆ ◆ ◆

Chapter 3

Reflecting

Our sixth president, John Quincy Adams, liked to swim nude each morning. The journalist Anne Royall had been trying in vain to interview Adams, so she went down to the bank of the Potomac River and sat on his clothes. She refused to get up and he was forced to reflect and answer her questions while keeping himself submerged. Reflection doesn't have to strip us bare or put us under duress, but we generally avoid it because we feel safer when we don't question our core beliefs, attitudes, and biases. **Examining truths we have long held dear can bring up significant anxiety.** So before looking at ways to develop reflection as a positive habit, we need to confront the potential roadblocks, and our own discomfort is at the top of the list.

Another significant challenge is that we value quick thinking above all else. This fits the fast-paced rhythm of business and society, where being busy and moving quickly are prized more than good judgment. The modern myth is that "fast is good and slow is bad," whatever the consequences. We reward a take-charge, action orientation, and so leaders believe it is better to "shoot first and ask questions later." Studies show leaders focus on immediately available data and solutions even when there is no time pressure and a systematic approach would yield a better result.[1]

Like in the story of the tortoise and the hare, stopping, reflecting, and focusing initially slow us down, but ultimately they make us more effective at getting to the goal. Moving too slow is obviously also risky. Effective leaders are impatient to make decisions and see results. Unfortunately, that impatience is often not paired with consideration for whether it is a good time to move slow or fast.

Fred was the director of sales for a consumer products company. He struggled to find time during the week to reflect. His day was jammed with meetings and in the evening he either had client events or tried to catch up on his backlog of email. As we looked closely at his schedule, Fred realized that Fridays were the only days he could count on for a quiet commute home. He now looks forward to his trip home each Friday and uses the time to reflect on his successes and lessons learned each week. He asks himself three questions:

+ "What am I focused on?"
+ "What am I learning?"
+ "Where am I taking my business?"

Experiment: Career Reflection

Think about all of the jobs you have had in your career, including your current one. For each job, think about the following questions:

1. What made you take the job?
2. How did it fit your skills, interests, and motivators?
3. What values did it allow you to express?
4. What did you learn from the job?
5. What career goal were you pursuing at that time? Why?

Our economy changes so rapidly that we all must continually reinvent ourselves and commit to lifelong learning. Reflect on how you have reinvented yourself through your career.

1. What themes emerge?
2. What ways do you want to reinvent yourself going forward?

◆ ◆ ◆

We can't just blame our leaders for not reflecting enough. Our unrealistic expectations for market returns drive organizations to measure and reward short-term tactical results, thus propelling a frenetic, unsustainable pace. Unfortunately, the resulting haphazard decision-making and lack of reflection is quite costly, as evidenced by the 2008 financial crisis. In contrast, companies that adopt a disciplined approach to decision-making have consistently better long-term returns.[2]

One of my clients, a large financial services firm, committed last year to over two hundred strategic initiatives. Through the course of the year they began to realize that their people were burning out and that it was impossible to execute on this many priorities at once. I helped them organize a meeting of their executives to decide what to stop doing and how to more effectively focus. After much discussion, they were able to set aside their egos and pet projects in order to make some tough decisions. They are now working to institute measures that help companies avoid falling back into this "acceleration trap":[3]

1. Clarify decision-making processes so that only high-value projects get approval.

2. Ask challenging questions of every potential new project:

   a. Do we have sufficient resources to succeed on this project?

   b. Who has the time to champion and own it?

   c. What will we deemphasize or stop doing to make room for this project?

3. Cap the number of goals that individuals and departments can take on.

4. On a regular basis, ask employees what the company should stop doing.

5. Institute extended time-outs from change so employees can think and recover.

The pressure to perform against short-term goals creates an environment where organizations do not reflect and so do not learn from mistakes. Just as reflection makes us uncomfortable individually, Chris Argyris found organizations create a variety of defensive postures to avoid examining failure because of the potential it has to bring up embarrassment, pain, and conflict.[4] Companies reward employees for taking the safe path — repeating the tried and true — rather than exploring new market opportunities or potential competitive threats.

In the 1960s and 1970s, U.S. automakers focused on competing with each other and largely ignored the Japanese threat on the low end of the market. By the 1980s the Japanese held a significant share of the *whole* market. Between 1980 and 1990 U.S. carmakers had to close thirteen North American plants while Japanese companies built eleven new North American plants. Unfortunately, U.S. automakers did not learn from this failure. From 2000 to 2010 they continued to focus on large trucks and vans while Japanese makers focused on more fuel-efficient models. When the recession hit and consumers wanted more fuel-efficient cars, U.S. automakers were not prepared. General Motors had to be bailed out of bankruptcy by the U.S. government.

We can improve performance by placing greater value on productive failure — i.e., on failure that we can learn from.[5] Organizations can do this by intentionally setting up experiments across departments and lines of business. Employees can be encouraged to continue experimenting rather than being punished for failing as is usually the case. In addition, because most experiments fail, we need to create systematic ways to capture the learning from these failures. Forums can be established to examine and disseminate learning across the organization. Off-sites, conferences, and training programs can serve this function well.

The urgency to move and think quickly is unparalleled during armed combat. To make sure soldiers learn even under these conditions, the U.S. Army instituted a discipline of after-action reviews. Every task and mission is followed by time for soldiers to look at actual versus intended results. The focus is on lessons each soldier can take away, as opposed to recommendations for others. Toward this end, guidelines for these reviews include involving everyone in the discussion and asking open-ended questions to "enable soldiers to discover for themselves what happened, why it happened, and how to sustain strengths and improve on weaknesses."[6] To bring together learning from these separate discussions, the army created the Center for Lesson Learned at Fort Leavenworth with opportunities for on-line and in-person training. Few organizations take learning from reflection so seriously.

Chapter 4

Learning
through Reflecting

Jared was a brilliant Mr. Fix-it. The CEO, Michelle, knew she could parachute Jared into any struggling business in their manufacturing conglomerate and he would set it straight. Jared loved the challenge of solving tough problems. He was a no-nonsense manager who people respected and feared. Not knowing who he could trust when he took over a new business, he took his own counsel and made quick decisions. After ten years of turning around businesses, the COO job opened up and Michelle tapped him for it.

Things did not go as expected. Jared's direct reports soon started complaining to Michelle. Jared was meddling in every function he managed. He couldn't stop himself from telling people what to do, even functional experts who had years of experience in their disciplines. His career had taught him that people are stupid and mess things up when left on their own. They needed direction and a kick in the pants. Michelle ultimately realized she couldn't keep protecting Jared and asked him to come see her.

One of the best teachers is a wide variety of challenging experiences. However, we do not always learn from experience. And like Jared, without support and guidance we often learn negative lessons. We hire college graduates with the best grades and test scores hoping that a high IQ will help employees learn on their own, but unfortunately IQ does not always predict who will learn. **Luckily we can learn how to learn.**[1] A central element in this process is reflecting on our approach to learning. This then enables us to modify our approach to fit each situation.

Experiment: Learning How to Learn

Learning can be thought of as a four-stage cycle:[2]

1. We start off with an *experience*.

2. We then step back and *reflect* on that experience.

3. Our reflection leads to a *conclusion* or insight about what we learned.

4. To complete the cycle we need to *plan* how we will apply or test out that insight in the future.

Learning through reflecting is like carrying out a series of small experiments.

LEARNING CYCLE

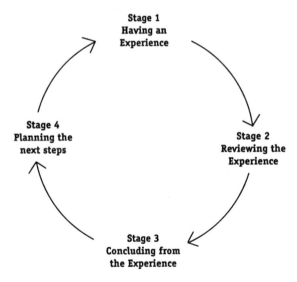

Each of us tends to have a preference for a part of the cycle or style of learning. Think about what you like to do most:

* *Activists* enjoy jumping in to new experiences
* *Reflectors* step back and review events

- *Theorists* make mental models and predictions
- *Pragmatists* plan how to apply new ideas

If you are like most executives, you are an experiential learner (an Activist). Unfortunately, without as much reflection or planning, you may not integrate your learning as well or be able to call on it in new situations.

- Given your style, is there a part of the learning cycle where you could spend more time?
- What kinds of things could you do to complement your current learning style?
- Are there people with different styles you could learn from?

◆ ◆ ◆

I worked with a leadership development executive, Caryn, who had the opposite problem from most leaders: she couldn't stop reflecting! Her ideas were innovative and elegant, but her style made it extremely difficult for her to make decisions or finish anything. The key is to know when you are stuck in one phase of the learning cycle, and to use a different mode to complete the process.

Balancing cycles of reflecting and experiencing makes us more effective learners.[3] It also makes our learning deeper, less superficial, and more enduring.[4] Think of a subject you know very well. Chances are you developed your expertise by reflecting on ideas, testing them out, and constructing your own frameworks. Now think of the courses you took in school. You were probably taught a passive approach to learning: you were told to listen quietly, memorize information, and recall on command. Most of that knowledge is now lost because theoretical categories are hard to integrate without applying them. We need real-world "messy" problems that we care about to make us reflect and actively create our own answers.[5]

Experiment: Journaling

A journal can help you reflect on and capture learning. A journal goes beyond a diary, which is simply a recording of experiences, events, stories, and anecdotes. A journal is a place to analyze the meaning contained in experiences.

As you try the experiments in this book, consider using a journal to reflect and record your learning. You may also want to write about specific incidents during your day that you want to look at more closely. The rhythm of writing at a regular time each day or week can make reflection a habit.

Start off with some of the following questions:

1. What did I do well this week? And not so well?

2. What did I learn?

3. How did I learn it?

4. How can I plan to apply the learning going forward?

5. What attitude am I taking toward myself and my learning? Am I pushing myself or being self-critical?

If you keep your journal private it can increase the safety and comfort of writing there and enable you to look more deeply into your assumptions, logic, and conclusions. A potential danger with private journals, though, is that they can reinforce introspection without objective reflection. Sharing some of your writing and ideas with a trusted thinking partner can help mitigate this issue and generate new insights.[6]

◆ ◆ ◆

Experiment: Forming a Personal Board of Directors

It is very hard to see your own behavior clearly. You need objective feedback and some distance from your ideas to gain clarity and accurate self-awareness. Reflection can be empty and self-deceptive without input from others.

Identify a group of advisors who can give you support, feedback, and counsel.[7] Think about people you trust, admire, and respect for their candor and business judgment. Ideally your board should have people with diverse backgrounds, experiences and thinking styles so you can get different perspectives. If you are going to make the best possible decisions, you want access to the best possible information and resources. Think about different categories of board members:

* *Thinking partners.* A thinking partner is a colleague or friend whose job is to listen and ask questions to help you think about specific issues, not to tell you what to do. Think about blocking out an hour every few weeks and offer to return the favor by splitting each meeting — you get thirty minutes, and your partner gets thirty minutes.

* *Allies.* An ally is someone you can count on for support when you need it. This can be emotional support, resources, or lobbying. Your ally understands what you are trying to accomplish, trusts your values, and can be counted on to back you.

* *Advocates.* An advocate, or sponsor, is someone who has a seat at the table and can put in a good word for you, for example, when promotion decisions are being made. Advocates know your skills and potential and are willing to expend their political capital on your behalf.

* *Mentors and coaches.* Mentors provide insider knowledge of companies, industries, and fields. They are usually people who have significant experience and can help you navigate your career path. Coaches are trained professionals who offer outsider objectivity and expertise on learning new behaviors and leadership skills.

Surround yourself with smart people, and then listen to them.
— *Rich Smith, Vice President of Human Resources,*
Kaiser Permanente

Forming a board is a way of expanding your network while also zeroing in on who will be the core. Use your first few board members to generate ideas for new additions. Realize potential board members may be wary of the commitment, so make sure to explain that you will ask for their support only when necessary and that you will respect their time.

◆ ◆ ◆

Jared was lucky. He was able to convince Michelle to give him time to address the feedback. Michelle also offered Jared a coach, but not being trusting, Jared took months to let his coach in. His coach, a skilled colleague of mine, Karen Muchnick, knew she needed not to push too hard. He was defensive, and his need to be right initially prevented him from looking at his own role in the problem. It was only when he started to feel that Karen accepted him and appreciated his strengths that he was able to begin to take responsibility and honestly reflect on what had happened.

Reflecting with Karen enabled Jared to begin to understand how he had learned the behavior that was getting in the way and how it impacted his team. He was able to make himself vulnerable enough to ask his direct reports for ongoing feedback as he experimented with a new approach to managing. Asking for their feedback bought him time and made his directs more open to the possibility that he could change.

Almost three years later, Jared is still the COO. He has adopted a more supportive management style, though he still occasionally slips back into old habits. Almost being removed from the COO position was scary for Jared and now serves as a powerful reminder of his need to listen to and support his team, and the danger of trying to be the smartest one in the room. He learned that going it alone as a leader is a sure way to fail, and so now he surrounds himself with people who help him reflect, get perspective, and complete his learning.

Chapter 5

Focusing

Keith was the lead graphic artist in a large advertising firm. He worked on the highest-profile assignments because of his superb ability to bring concepts to life in pictures. Though few knew it, he was quite insecure, and his creative ability was the largest source of his self-esteem (followed closely by his black belt in karate).

One morning Sheila, Keith's colleague in the production department, brought him a drawing and showed him a mistake she found. He stared at her silently and took the drawing. Sheila went back to her desk, thinking everything was fine. After all, Keith was known for being somewhat reserved and hard to read. A few minutes later Keith followed Sheila back to her office and kicked her door down. Keith's HR person asked me if I could give him some "anger management coaching." I started with Keith by teaching him to focus and breathe.

Focusing is choosing how and where you pay attention. Consciously paying attention is like directing a spotlight. The challenge is to learn to point the light where you want. The spotlight is helpful in seeing what is going on inside and around you. You begin learning to use it by directing it toward yourself. When I first started to work with Keith he did not know how to direct his spotlight inward, and so he did not know when his anger was being triggered. Keith needed to learn mindfulness techniques to pick on inner cues that told him his anger was being triggered, and then learn strategies like mindful breathing to settle his inner turmoil so he could more rationally figure out what to do.

You can direct your spotlight in three ways: scope (narrow or wide attention), time (past or present), and attitude (critical or accepting). It is best to start developing your ability to focus and concentrate by attending narrowly to the present moment. With practice you can choose to focus narrowly (e.g., on one particular person in front of you) or widely (on a team's nonverbal signals at a meeting) depending on the situation. Mindfulness adds the importance of an open-minded, accepting attitude.

It is important to distinguish an accepting attitude from fatalism, complacency, passivity, or laziness. Acceptance means looking squarely at reality rather than pretending or being in denial. Acceptance did not mean giving Keith permission to give in to his anger. It meant facing himself honestly, with all his skills and imperfections. Keith needed to learn to do this without fear that being vulnerable and open would drag him into self-pity.

Once you accept what is you can then work more effectively toward specific objectives and improve your circumstances. Being able to look at what makes you uncomfortable enables you to develop self-awareness. Behaviors that can derail your career are called "blind spots" because they are areas where you don't want to look. Keith's blind spot was his pride. When this was challenged, he tried to protect his self-esteem with rage. Cultivating self-acceptance enabled Keith to look directly at his pride and the function it served in propping up his sense of self.

Acceptance also implies an attitude of kindness. Here too we need to be careful, because we often mistakenly associate being a friend to ourselves and self-care with selfishness and self-indulgence. As a result, we end up pushing ourselves and undermining our development with self-criticism. Keith was so sensitive to his colleague's criticism because he was raw from constant self-criticism. Keith was able to cultivate the antidote: an attitude of openness, welcoming, and curiosity toward himself.

Experiment: Programming Mindful Breathing

The breathing exercise I introduced in the overview is a terrific way to cultivate mindfulness. However, it is difficult to remember to check in with yourself and bring your attention back to your breathing during the rush of the day. The trick is to find natural cues that work for you. Keith programmed his PDA screen saver so that every time he turned it on it read:

     – Am I breathing?

     – Am I smiling?

     – What is my attitude toward myself?

- Next time the phone rings, become aware of how your breathing quickens. Emails and phone calls trigger a fight-or-flight stress response — increased heart rate, a spike in blood pressure and shallow respiration. You can reprogram this into a relaxation response.[1] When you hear the phone ring, stop what you are doing and turn away from your computer. On the second ring, take a breath. On the third ring, smile — notice the affect of smiling on your attitude. Now pick up the phone.

- Find additional reminders for yourself like a Post-it note on your desk or small dot on your watch. Try paying attention to your breathing during your commute, whenever you ride an elevator, or when you touch a doorknob. Changing gears as you go from one meeting to the next can be an important way to recenter your attention and clear your mind.

- The more you practice being aware of your breath, the stronger this connection will become and the easier it will be to find this safety net when you need it.

◆ ◆ ◆

The Middlesex University master's program in executive coaching teaches coaching to candidates in companies across the United States. Since 2003 it has been the only program to offer an accredited graduate degree in executive coaching in this country. During the first few years after I developed the program I would bring the faculty together once every six weeks to review student progress and brainstorm the best ways to teach the demanding work-based curriculum. We began each meeting by first putting away our Blackberries. Then we sat in silence for a minute of mindful breathing, pulling ourselves out of the clutter of our thoughts and feelings. When I saw people look up, we broke the silence and did a check-in.

Our check-ins made sure everyone's voice was in the room before we started the meeting. They could be unexpectedly valuable. At one meeting a senior faculty member talked about how glad he was to be there because he had narrowly avoided getting run off the road by a tractor trailer on the way in. His check-in immediately brought a tone of gratitude and appreciation to the meeting. Starting meetings by breathing and focusing helped us be more connected and productive as a team.

Experiment: Meditation

One of the best ways to develop your ability to focus is meditation. This practice brings the distractions of your mind into stark relief. As you may have found in the mindful breathing exercise, it can seem quite loud in your head when you stop moving. However, once you learn not to lose yourself in thinking, meditation can be very relaxing and energizing.

Meditation is not doing. However, simply sitting (or lying down) and just being for any period is next to impossible when you start. Therefore, it can be helpful to bring in a measure of *intention* (doing) into what is in a pure sense just *attention* (being). You can do this by focusing your attention on images, objects, sounds, or physical sensations. Of all of these, your breath is one of the best anchors for your attention.

- Mindfulness meditation is simply staying still and breathing mindfully. Every time your attention wanders, simply bring it back to your breathing. Start with five minutes a couple of times a week. If you feel like doing more, you can build up to twenty or thirty minutes, but there is no perfect length, and any amount of time is healing. Notice the impact on your mental clarity of meditating regularly. You may even notice you need less sleep.

- Thoughts have such a powerful pull that when you start meditating you can spend most of your time just bringing your attention back to your breathing. Each time you refocus, try to smile to yourself and bring your attention back with gentleness and acceptance rather than force. Notice any self-criticism and try to replace it with welcoming and curiosity. Cultivating a kinder, more patient and open attitude toward yourself is a large part of meditation. With these attitudes mindfulness gets you out of your head, and in some ways it could better be described as "heartfulness."

A common misconception is that meditating is trying to stop yourself from thinking. This is actually counterproductive. What you are really doing is learning to turn your attention away from thinking. In time, your thinking will slow down and have less pull on you, but not if you make this a goal. Your brain is an anticipation and explanation machine. It is programmed to think ahead and make stories about what you experience, which makes it more difficult to stay present and just take in what is. Accepting your brain's natural function can help you not to get frustrated with yourself for continually thinking when you are meditating.

There are a number of meditation techniques besides mindfulness meditation. One of the most researched approaches is to repeat a mantra — a word or phrase, such as "peace" or "one." If your religious or spiritual tradition includes prayer, then that may be the best focus point for your meditation. It can be tempting to dabble and experiment with many techniques, but you will get more from finding one that works for you and sticking with it. If mindfulness meditation does not feel like a good fit, Tara Brach provides a good overview of alternatives in her book *Radical Acceptance*.[2]

◆ ◆ ◆

Two years after we had finished our coaching, I got a honeymoon postcard from Keith. It showed him and his wife joyful and happy together on the beach. He wrote that he was still meditating, and while he sometimes forgot, he had found ways to remind himself to breathe at work. He had not lost his cool or used his karate on anyone. His postcard made my day.

Experiment: Walking Meditation

It is hard to stop the busyness of life in order to meditate even for just a few minutes. And yet formal meditation in a quiet room is easier than bringing mindfulness into the midst of other activities. Practicing mindfulness in action is essential to carrying over the learning from meditation and reaping its full benefits. In addition to creating reminders for yourself to breathe mindfully during the course of the day, an excellent way to practice mindfulness in action is walking meditation.

- ◆ Walking meditation is just walking, being aware of your footsteps, and breathing mindfully. Whenever you find yourself daydreaming or getting caught by what is around you, simply bring your attention back to the sensation of your feet softly meeting the ground and your breath moving in and out. Walking meditation is particularly useful if you find you get restless or sleepy during mindfulness meditation. Start by practicing slowly at home — counting one or even two breaths per step. Out in the street take a natural pace, and count how many steps per breath feel right.

For a number of weeks a colleague of mine, Ann, had been feeling dizzy. Her doctors could offer no medical explanation, other than that she was under a lot of stress at work. I suggested Ann try walking meditation, and she started practicing on her way to the office each morning. This was quite a challenge given that she lived in the middle of a large city. She found it was a wonderful way to bring some peace to her commute and she arrived at work in a much more centered and grounded frame of mind. She has kept up the practice, and her dizziness has not reappeared.

◆ ◆ ◆

Focusing mindfully is different from reflecting. Reflection looks retrospectively at your thoughts and actions, their impact and your learning process. Mindfulness turns attention to your ongoing stream of thoughts, emotions, physical sensations, and attitudes. **Reflection is *intentional and goal-directed:* there is something you are trying to accomplish, solve, or improve. Mindfulness is *attentional and neutral:* rather than focusing on problems, you objectively observe yourself, your reactions, and external stimuli without judgment.** You try to avoid saying, "This is good, that is bad," or "This is helpful, and that harmful." You are simply witnessing and staying present with what is. This means not doing and not intending.

Focusing is a priceless tool. To use it productively you first need to stop and steady your spotlight. You do this by reminding yourself to breathe and check in with your body. You then clean and polish your lens with mindfulness practices like meditation. You charge your battery, the energy for focusing, by cultivating a positive attitude toward yourself. You can then use your attention to identify obstacles, learn, and solve problems.

Chapter 6

Learning through Focusing

The ability to learn quickly is a key predictor of leadership success.[1] Research suggests that most agile learners are:

- Reflective and continually examine themselves and their effectiveness
- Curious, driven to learn and committed to self-development
- Open-minded and have no shame about not being the expert
- Willing to take risks, make mistakes, and look stupid
- Experimenters who enjoy tinkering and improving processes and products
- Flexible, adaptable, and comfortable with ambiguity

Applying mindfulness to learning enables you to develop these characteristics.

Traditional mindfulness training initially asks you to stop moving and focus inward. This helps you tune in to the messages coming from your gut feelings and intuitions, direct your attention where you want, and tame the constant movement of your mind. To complement this, you begin to develop mindfulness toward your external environment. Rather than turning your attention away from distractions as in mindful breathing and meditation, the goal here is to see and feel more. You do this by actively looking for new information and subtle distinctions around you. This enables you to learn faster and to become more effective communicating, building relationships, and leading teams.

Experiment: Tiger Eye Meditation

One way to start turning mindfulness toward your environment is by meditating with your eyes open. The basic instructions are the same.

36

Follow your breathing, and use this as an anchor. However, now do it with your eyes half open, like a tiger. Pick a spot in front of you and slightly below eye level to focus your gaze. Your attention is divided between your internal experience and external stimuli. Notice how this feels in contrast to closed-eye meditation. Though it can be harder to focus inward, it can be easier to stay alert and wakeful when meditating this way.

◆ ◆ ◆

Experiment: Noticing Distractions

The biggest challenge with mindfulness is remembering to practice it. There are so many things that grab our attention, and when you are in the midst of tasks and pushing toward goals, it is supremely difficult to step back and refocus. It can help to use little cracks and openings between activities to turn on your attention. See if you can use some of these moments to notice the patterns in what attracts and distracts you.

- Distractions: Notice what kinds of things hook your attention and cause it to shift. How long can you work before you need a break?

- Environment: Study what things around you keep you engaged. Are you sensitive to noise, or do you prefer to have activity in the background?

- Food: Notice your energy and ability to focus right after meals. See how this varies depending on what and how much you eat or drink. What kinds of foods make you more or less focused?

- Technology: Pay attention to the draw of TV screens, monitors, the Internet, and email. How much time do you spend on these? How do you feel after watching TV for more than thirty minutes? Many people feel tired, angry, and depressed after watching TV for an extended time. What would it be like to drop TV for a few days, a week, or more?

- Try to stay in touch with your body at the same time as you are noticing distractions around you. Shift your attention back and forth between focusing internally and externally.

- Record your observations in your journal.

◆ ◆ ◆

In order to notice information you need to actively change your perspective. If you are looking at a product, you can walk around it to view it from multiple angles. Giving the product to a customer can introduce you to a completely different perspective. You can also experiment with alternative ways to frame experiences, which can radically alter their meaning. For example, if you see the loss of a job as a disaster, you will likely feel bad about yourself and depressed. If you decide to see it as a new opportunity, you will likely feel excited and challenged. Having a positive attitude is in large part about the way you choose to frame events.

Experiment: Mindful Reading

As you read the rest of this chapter, see if you can apply a mindful attitude. If a concept or experiment seems strange or does not match your experience, see if you can hold off before rejecting it. Try to view it from multiple perspectives and vantage points. Explore whether your reaction is based on a previous negative experience, and reflect on whether your conclusion from that experience is still valid.

If you feel yourself getting bored, rather than turning off your attention, see if you can actively look for something new or unexpected in the section. Consider your attitude toward learning, and notice if your goal is to find truths or answers that exist outside yourself. You will learn much more if you use what you find to create your own meaning and perspectives.

◆ ◆ ◆

Like many bright professionals, Jennifer was rewarded for becoming an expert. After fifteen years of building trade support systems for the credit default swap business at her investment company, she knew more than anyone about how to settle and account for these complex financial transactions. Senior traders relied on her expertise and made sure she was taken care of at bonus time.

Hiding out in back office operations had an element of security in this highly competitive Wall Street firm. However, she attracted the attention of her managers, who recognized her potential and wanted to give her more responsibilities. She resisted, giving different excuses that never really made sense to them.

After we conducted an initial assessment of her skills, I asked her to think about why her managers made various decisions. As we dissected each maneuver she became more curious about the power plays above her. Rather than denigrating the behavior as manipulative, we looked at multiple perspectives and how each party had acted to further their own or their department's political interests. Managers were using their influence to establish their teams' boundaries, create group identities, get more resources, and clarify roles between departments. They all had their own agendas, but as we reflected these started to make sense to her, and to intrigue her.

I suggested she seek out mentors and she began to experiment with learning from people who knew about different products and areas of the business. We started to get feedback that she was coming across as less arrogant and condescending. A lateral move opened up and her boss offered her the role. I encouraged Jennifer to consider the challenge of managing a group where she would not be the expert. She was hesitant, and asked her boss if she could take the weekend to think it over.

In some ways our biological wiring helps us to be more mindful of our environment. Our attention is naturally attracted to novelty and movement. Like barracudas, we love to chase bright, shiny things. However, the allure of stimulation and variety is a double-edged sword. It can give you a buzz that wakes you up but can quickly become addictive. We call Blackberries "Crackberries" for good reason — once you start using them you have trouble putting them down. Soon you can have difficulty screening out information and concentrating when you need to.

Clearly you cannot give your attention to everything equally, especially given the information overload of our culture. You must learn to ignore irrelevant details. Habituation is the adaptive habit of tuning out information you don't care about.[2] For example, living in New York City for the past eighteen years, I gradually became habituated to the regular sounds of airplanes flying overhead.

When allowed to go too far, though, habituation can lead you to screen out important information. Before you know it you are on automatic pilot. You have stopped questioning old assumptions and beliefs, and are applying out-of-date strategies and approaches. Acting mindlessly you are less flexible and able to learn.

Habituation can also mean you get less enjoyment from activities and become harder to satisfy. Getting bored more easily, you look for the next most exciting material possession, experience, or relationship. You can also habituate to having dozens of things going on at once. You stop noticing that you are not present, and you reinforce the habit of distraction.[3]

In order to combat habituation you can cultivate "beginner's mind." This is the perspective of the beginner, of not knowing, rather than pretending you know. By becoming aware of and questioning your preconceived notions you can start to open your mind to new information.

In the beginner's mind there are infinite possibilities,
in the expert's mind there are few.   —*Shunryu Suzuki*

Beginner's mind is fundamentally an attitude of humility and openness. Assuming you know is a posture of arrogance that gets in the way of learning. This stance is a false pride you adopt when you are feeling unworthy or unintelligent and want to prove yourself to be "one-up." However, if you can actively adopt a "one-down" position, information and learning naturally flow toward you, like water flowing downhill.

I learned the value of the one-down position from a former boss. I was just out of graduate school, while he had years of experience and insights. Whenever we talked, if he sensed I was about to say something, he would abruptly interrupt himself in order to listen. Sometimes this was quite frustrating because, after I spoke, I realized I was much more interested in what he was about to say than whatever ended up coming out of my mouth. He explained the rationale for this behavior very simply. "When I'm talking, I'm not learning."

Along with beginner's mind, sensitization is a process of reawakening your attention in order to refresh your attitude and undo the effects of habituation. Sensitization increases your awareness, sometimes abruptly and not always helpfully. After 9/11, I suddenly became aware again of airplanes flying overhead. Now, even years later, I, along with many

New Yorkers, turn my head quickly when I hear the sound of a low-flying airplane.

Experiment: Positive Sensitization

Positive sensitization is intentionally applying mindfulness to a particular subject. It is making the decision to fully enjoy and savor an experience, which over time elevates your mood and sense of well-being. Research also demonstrates that when you approach learning and problem-solving with this attitude of open interest you are more effective.[4]

- If you work in an office, the experience of being outdoors in natural settings can be an excellent way to come back to your senses.[5] In the woods or at the beach you immediately notice sights, sounds and smells that you have been missing.

- You can sensitize yourself in a park or backyard by lying down with your head near the grass. Notice each blade of grass and how each one is a slightly different shade of green.[6]

- Find a tree and look up. Notice the intricate patterns made by the branches and leaves. Take a moment to breathe mindfully and tune in to how your body feels.

◆ ◆ ◆

Experiment: Ultradian Rhythms and Changing Channels

As much as you build your capacity to attend, you need to periodically change your mental channel to stay fresh. In addition to your daily circadian rhythm, you have a ninety-minute ultradian rhythm that can help you know when you need a break. Every ninety minutes your body goes through a period of greater alertness and activity, followed by a period of lower energy and decreased focus. When you feel yourself going into one of these troughs, it can be helpful to take a minute to reset.[7] A short pit stop can have a tremendous impact on your subsequent ability to focus and solve problems creatively.

- We have a number of mental and emotional channels as alternatives to our usual verbal analytical mode.[8] The simplest option is to just get up from your desk and talk with people. Having a water cooler or coffee pantry in the office provides an easy way to take a social break.

- You can experiment with more dynamic options like drawing or doodling, stretching, walking around the block, or playing music.

- Try giving yourself permission to daydream for a minute while staring out the window.

- Take two minutes, and count as you breathe slowly: "1, 2, 3..." as you breathe in. Then count "1, 2, 3..." as you breathe out. You may find counting can help you focus and get out of your head.

- Experiment with which channels work best and look for rituals that can remind you to change gears.

◆ ◆ ◆

An important way to increase your openness and learning agility is to seek out new experiences and challenges. Leaders learn the most from stretch assignments and unfamiliar roles that demand new skills, perspectives and approaches.[9] This is not to say we cannot learn from courses and books. However, the most meaningful learning comes from experience, provided the experience is in a setting where there is constructive feedback, support, and time for reflection. Successful leaders do not wait for new challenges to be handed to them. They actively seek out developmental roles, change jobs frequently, and say yes whenever there is a new opportunity.[10] Of course, this can also lead to overcommitment if they are not thoughtful about each choice and why they are saying yes.

Jennifer said yes to the new assignment she was offered. However, initially she struggled in the role. She was not sure what she should be doing in meetings if it was not giving the answer. She had to learn to facilitate and coach her team rather than directing the action. Though she lacked expertise in the new product area, she could teach her people how to think and take a disciplined approach to problem-solving. After a few months she started to enjoy the freedom and greater time for strategic thinking that came with this new way of leading. She also enjoyed learning about the details of her new product, but she stopped short of becoming the expert again. She instead focused on learning to anticipate her impact in relationships, developing a broader network across the firm, and influencing more effectively by reading her peers' agendas.

Learning through reflection and learning through focusing complement each other. You learn through reflection by looking backward and then forward. Looking back at your experiences enables you to uncover what and how you learned. You give new meaning to experience, and especially when you reflect with others, find new perspectives and information you had overlooked. Looking forward then enables you to experiment with your new insights. Learning through focusing is primarily present-focused. It depends on your managing the influence of distractions on your attention, and balancing the effects of habituation and sensitization. You actively change perspectives and channels, and use beginner's mind to stay open to new experiences. Together, reflection and focusing help you become a more agile and adaptable learner. They also enable you to master the MindShifts that are the heart of becoming more effective as a professional and a leader.

Part II

A Map, a Compass, and Seven Essential Skills

Overview

Part I gave you the foundations of stopping, reflecting, and focusing your attention. You also understand how to use these to accelerate learning. Now we will apply these skills to learning essential leadership skills. So many things seem important to learn as a leader, it is important to have a way to sort through them. "MindShifts" provide you with a map to navigate this territory. These are a set of seven attentional shifts you need to make as you go from managing yourself to managing a large organization. The MindShifts also serve as a self-assessment as you create an initial plan for your development. Values and purpose are your inner compass that tells you if you are on track. Each of the remaining chapters is devoted to a specific leadership skill. I provide examples and experiments to show you where to focus to learn strategic and innovative thinking, communication, relationship building and negotiating, stress management and resilience, emotional intelligence, and leading and developing teams.

Chapter 7

MindShifting

Wendy is a senior executive who started her career as an administrative assistant. Her first role was in a branch office of a multinational financial services company. She was a fast learner with a great deal of energy and the ability to get things done. She was steadily given greater responsibility. She began managing the administrative staff in her office and then took on the compliance and business management functions as well. Her skills and service orientation got the attention of the district manager, who picked her to run these functions for the region. After just a few years she was promoted to headquarters to run administration, compliance, and business management nationally.

I met Wendy shortly after she started her role at headquarters. She was scattered during our conversation and would take phone calls and check email every few minutes. She told me she was frustrated and struggling with the huge volume of work. It seemed every compliance issue in the field would bubble up to her because she knew the most and was the best at solving difficult problems. Her days were filled with back-to-back meetings because everyone wanted her time. She began falling behind on deadlines and would often be twenty or thirty minutes late to meetings. She would apologize profusely but was not really aware of how destructive her behavior was becoming on her relationships and reputation. As much as she was drowning, she felt like the go-to expert. She enjoyed seeing her own impact and so it was hard for her to delegate real authority to her staff.

As Wendy moved from each level to the next, she needed to change where she focused, what she valued, and how she defined her job. These changes can be described as a series of MindShifts as you go from individual contributor to leader.[1] Wendy was ultimately able to see how she had become a bottleneck because she was stuck on the first MindShift, Doing to Leading. By learning to reflect and focus she was able to shift her attention from getting things done on her own to developing her team and facilitating their work. Her job was no longer to assemble the budget and double-check it herself. It was to make sure the right people came together so the budget reflected her whole department's needs and goals.

Wendy also became more aware of her impact and better at setting boundaries, including saying "no" to problems that were not hers to solve. This gave her more time to think about how to improve her department's performance. After a few years she mastered several more MindShifts and was ready for another opportunity. Wendy is now running a rapidly growing business that is central to her company's future.

There are seven fundamental MindShifts as you go from managing yourself to managing organizations (see the chart on the next page).

Experiment: Self-Assessment and Initial Development Planning

The MindShifts can serve as a self-assessment and roadmap as you plan your development. Moving from left to right along each dimension requires a change in how you prioritize and evaluate your success. First consider the "doing to leading" MindShift.

1. Place an "X" where you feel your skills and focus are currently on the continuum.

2. Place "O" where you would like to see yourself in the future given your current role as well as the requirements of future potential roles.

3. Assess where you are and where you would like to be for the rest of the MindShifts.

SEVEN MINDSHIFTS

MANAGING YOURSELF . . . . **MANAGING ORGANIZATIONS**

Doing . . . . **Leading**

Accomplishing tasks on your own

Influencing, negotiating, facilitating, and conceptualizing

———————————————————————————→

Exchanging Information . . . . **Communicating**

Giving and receiving information about your own activities

Creating a two-way dialogue with a wide constituent group about your organization's activities and your future plan, vision, and brand

———————————————————————————→

Relationship Building . . . . **Networking**

Building individual relationships with teammates, customers, and supervisors

Building a broad network of relationships with subordinates, peers, customers, superiors, vendors, board members, community and government representatives

———————————————————————————→

Self-Development . . . . **Coaching and Team Development**

Working toward your own personal and professional growth

Selecting, delegating, motivating, and developing others

———————————————————————————→

Personal Accountability . . . . **Organizational Accountability**

Monitoring your own work processes, deadlines and goals

Measuring the organization's success (profit, efficiency, quality, service); allocating and brokering resources

———————————————————————————→

Task Analysis . . . . **Market Analysis**

Problem-solving the best way to accomplish a task

Deciding what business to be in, a vision for where it should go, and strategies to to get there

———————————————————————————→

Self-Awareness . . . . **Interpersonal Awareness**

Knowing the strengths and weaknesses of your style

Managing your emotions and behaviors and their impact on others

———————————————————————————→

I reference the relevant MindShifts in subsequent chapters and provide examples of how to refocus your attention to master each. In light of your self-assessment, you may want to focus on the following chapters that relate to specific MindShifts. **Successfully navigating each MindShift depends on developing the underlying competencies referenced below.**

Doing   **Leading**

➔

Chap. 8 Values and Purpose
Chap. 17 Perfectionism, Self-Criticism, and Self-Confidence
Chap. 19 Tolerating Uncertainty and Change

Exchanging Information   **Communicating**

➔

Chap.12 Communication

➔

Relationship Building   **Networking**

➔

Chap. 13 Emotional Intelligence
Chap. 14 Relationship Building, Negotiating, and Networking

Self-Development   **Coaching and Team Development**

➔

Chap. 12 Communication
Chap. 15 Leading and Developing Teams
Chap. 24 Mindful Coaching

Personal Accountability   **Organizational Accountability**

➔

Chap. 9 Strategic Thinking
Chap. 21 Prioritization and Time Management
Chap. 22 Goal-Setting and Development Planning
Chap. 23 Organizational Goals and Focus

Task Analysis   **Market Analysis**

➔

Chap. 9 Strategic Thinking
Chap. 10 Innovative Thinking
Chap. 23 Organizational Goals and Focus

Self-Awareness   **Interpersonal Awareness**

➔

Chap. 11 Stress Management and Resilience
Chap. 12 Communication
Chap. 13 Emotional Intelligence
Chap. 14 Relationship Building, Negotiating, and Networking

As you read each chapter, highlight the skills that are relevant for the MindShifts you feel are most important for your role and where you have the largest development gaps. This will help you build a pragmatic development plan.

A development plan is a commitment to:

1. Objectives: what you want to accomplish for yourself and your business. Wendy's objectives were to develop into a broader leader and grow her business.

2. Strategies: broad categories of skills (such as MindShifts) you want to develop. Beside going from doer to leader, Wendy needed to develop along the second MindShift, regarding communication. She had to shift from trying to quickly exchange small bits of information to creating a dialogue with a large group of people about her vision.

3. Tactics: the specific skills you want to develop and behaviors you want to target within each strategy. To communicate more effectively, Wendy needed to learn to quiet her mind and stay focused during conversations. This required her to practice mindfulness and listening exercises.

4. Measures: how you will know you are successful. Wendy's measures included bottom-line business impact, improved team efficiency, greater self-confidence, and positive feedback from her colleagues.

A development plan can serve as a reminder and a focusing tool. It can also be a good way to communicate your goals and means to solicit feedback and support. Do not try to write all the elements of your plan at this point. Simply begin thinking about your overall objectives, and then write down the potential strategies and tactics you would like to include as you read. The goal-setting chapter at the beginning of Part IV has a sample and additional advice on creating plans. When you get to that point, you should have enough information to complete a first draft. Realize that building a plan is an ongoing process and that you will continually evolve your plan as you go.

◆ ◆ ◆

Chapter 8

Values and Purpose

The importance of values-centered leadership has been highlighted by the many high-profile scandals of the last several years.[1] It is not just a few powerful and infamous leaders who are ethically challenged. We all face daily conflicts between organizational demands, client pressures, and the desire to protect our job.

Carlos was in what he felt was a no-win dilemma. He was head of sales in a software technology company that had gone through a long drought. His firm was about to launch a new product. The chief engineer, Dave, came to Carlos privately and told him that it would take a few months after the launch to work all the bugs out. Dave was not sure, but thought most users would not have significant problems. Carlos knew his salespeople had strong relationships with many customers who trusted the company and could use the software. He also knew a competitor was close to launching a product with similar features. Keeping his salespeople positive and motivated was very important to getting sales. If he mentioned the possible bugs his people could be paralyzed. But if he didn't mention them, it could hurt the relationship his salespeople had with customers over the long term.

Reflecting on your values makes your choices clearer. There are natural tensions between your values, and acknowledging them is essential to maintaining your integrity. Articulating your values and purpose also helps you clarify your long-range goals. **When your values are aligned with your goals you put more effort behind them, are more successful in achieving them, and feel a greater sense of well-being as you work toward them.**[2]

Experiment: Clarifying Values

List all the values that are important to you. Consider autonomy, power, control, structure, integrity, challenge, nurturing, family, security, balance, wealth, location, culture, personal growth, expertise, and recognition. Rank the list from the most to the least important. Rate how you actually act rather than making it a wish list. What changes would you make in your rankings or your behavior to align more closely with your values?

◆ ◆ ◆

Carlos reflected on his values, which included integrity, directness and long-term relationships. He decided he needed to inform his salespeople and customers that there might be a problem. He also realized that he and Dave needed to let their management know what was going on. Dave was initially unhappy about this because it was potentially embarrassing. However, Carlos needed to get senior management's support in case the problem turned out to be bigger than Dave anticipated. Carlos told his salespeople to inform customers that the risks were probably small, but that if any customer experienced an issue they would fix the problem or provide a full refund plus a credit toward a future purchase. The problem turned out to be isolated to a few customers as Dave thought, but Carlos's approach bought him more loyalty from all his customers who appreciated his honesty and vulnerability.

Corporate leadership development programs sometimes try to incorporate a focus on values, purpose, and alignment. This can take the form of small group discussions or reflective essays where employees describe their life purpose and how this connects with the organization's five-year plan. While an employee's purpose may seem a long way away from their day-to-day work, it need not be so disconnected, and such existential questions can actually make a lot of business sense. If our personal values and purpose align with the organization's mission there is a much greater chance the organization will be able to mobilize our energy and succeed. In fact, organizations whose employees understand and embrace the corporate mission, goals, and values enjoy a 29 percent greater return than other firms.[3]

Unfortunately, once leadership programs are over, organizations typically struggle to get people to continue the habit of reflection. Reflection is often left to the end of programs, where participants' attention is at its lowest. In addition, once the program is over, there is little follow up. Thinking about purpose becomes overshadowed by the press of the organization's short-term goals. The discipline of reflection ends up not being integrated into employees' objectives or ways of working.

Diageo is the largest spirits, wine, and beer company in the world. It is best known for its brands, such as Baileys, Guinness, and Smirnoff. Diageo picked its top nine hundred executives globally for a year-long leadership program incorporating multiple week-long events and intensive one-on-one coaching.

The participants in the Diageo program created a written description of their life purpose and shared this with their colleagues and teams. They were then asked to connect this purpose with the overall Diageo purpose of "Celebrating Life, Every Day, Everywhere." Many participants realized their purpose centered on developing others and helping them become successful, both at home and at work. In addition, each participant wrote a "leadership possibility." This was a story written four or five years in the future that looked back on accomplishments and growth over that time. Participants envisioned their "best self," imagining the leadership breakthroughs they achieved and resultant impact on the business.

In designing our program we made sure to put the powerful questions up front. Particularly given our ambitious goals and the turbulent business environment, the danger was that leaders would feel overwhelmed by the challenges they faced. Thus, we needed to keep leaders focused on making an immediate impact while maintaining their confidence in the possible.

—*Jade Starrett, Leadership Program Director, Diageo*

As I coached participants in the Diageo program I saw the tremendous impact of these exercises. The activities embedded the spirit of reflection, optimism, and creative thinking into the DNA of the organization. Diageo is just starting to collect return on investment data. Early indications are that the company's employee engagement scores went up 14 percent during the course of the program. This is the largest single year increase Diageo has ever experienced.

Experiment: Envisioning Purpose

Considering the top five values from the previous experiment, write a brief (one- or two-sentence) description of your purpose. What gives your life meaning? What do you want your life to have been about? What do you want your personal and professional legacy to be?

◆ ◆ ◆

Aligning your values and behavior can help prevent the potential negative impact of "insincere reflection."[4] Senior executives often feel a great deal of pressure not to make the wrong decision and so hire well recognized consulting firms. The hypocrisy of their analysis is often obvious to employees — the real goal is to justify the senior executive's decision and give him cover. If something goes wrong later he says, "Well, I hired [fill in your favorite firm], and they confirmed our new strategy and organizational design."

Another type of insincere reflection occurs when executives feel the need to show they are being facilitative and inclusive, but are not really interested in dialogue. A town hall will be held ostensibly to share ideas, but it quickly becomes clear to the participants that divergent views are not welcome. This is extremely demotivating to employees. The message is, "We are not interested in your perspective because it is uninformed and you don't have enough experience or seniority to add anything meaningful." Essentially, we have no confidence in your intellect or ability.

Companies often engage in exercises they hope will create a set of inspiring values statements. Most of these are written by senior executives because it is quicker. A few enlightened organizations recognize the importance of bottom-up processes that get the entire workforce involved and try hard to have the ultimate values statement represent a consensus view. However, they then struggle to have these statements become a reality. Part of the difficulty is that the final statements are so abstract that no one can translate them into action.

Another difficulty is that senior management is half-hearted in their commitment to the effort. They would like the company to be seen as values-based, and hope the plaque on the wall will be how the company is viewed. They support values work as essentially a public relations effort — they want to win awards like Fortune magazine's "100 Best Companies to Work For." So leaders go along, but don't really trust the connection between values and profits.

There is a growing body of research suggesting companies that invest in talent and cultural development are the highest performing by a range of measures including total shareholder return, return on equity, return on investment, market share, sales growth and innovation.[5] The pathway is increases in employee performance/attitudes result in increases in customer satisfaction, which in turn increases profitability. In addition, a number of socially conscious investment funds have started to outperform other funds.[6] These funds invest in companies with positive employment practices and screen out companies based on negative factors. The negative factors include practices that got companies in trouble during the 2008 financial crisis, including lax corporate governance, predatory lending, insufficient transparency, and executive pay not tied to performance.

Experiment: Living Values

I dream of an organization where the corporate mission on the wall is a living reality. Here are some characteristics of a company where I would be inspired to work:

- Everyone is encouraged to challenge the status quo and continuously improve processes, services, and products.

- People have fun and are not afraid of joking around with each other.

- Creative ideas are recognized and rewarded.

- Employees feel a sense of purpose and are proud to represent their corporation, its products, and the positive environment they help to create.

Think about your ideal organization and list its four most important features. How closely does your current organization fit this picture? How could you help your organization become a place you could live your values?

◆ ◆ ◆

Creating environments where employees can live their values is the most effective way to attract, retain, and develop people. However, with all the pressure toward expediency and survival, corporate values need to be continually discussed, recognized, and rewarded to become a set of real cultural practices and behaviors. The time and effort required challenge the basic premise of most organizations: **to what extent are we here to make profit and to what extent are we here to serve human needs?**

Chapter 9

Strategic Thinking

Sally was polished and sophisticated. She spoke several languages, having spent years in her fashion company's European stores and operations. She also knew her products and customers intimately. She was asked to return to take on a significantly larger role running all U.S. stores. Her boss Jeff realized it would take her time to get to know the unique field culture in the United States. As he reflected on her first six months, though, he realized she had a problem. She spent a great deal of time in the field, and it was terrific that she wanted to get to know each store and give her attention to front-line employees. However, Sally's district managers were complaining that she was meddling and trying to do their jobs. They had no sense of overall direction or where she wanted to take the business.

As Sally and I analyzed how she spent her time, it became clear that she had little opportunity to think strategically. When she was not traveling, she was swamped with issues that had piled up at the home office. To get on top of these she spent all day in back-to-back meetings and then tried to follow up with email in the evenings. She needed to trust that she had done enough homework about the current state in the field and that her team could handle day-to-day issues. She had to break her attention away from the tactical To-Do list in front of her to look ahead and see the big picture.

Strategic thinking is one of the hardest skills for leaders to develop. It does not require genius, just focus. Having clarified your values and purpose, you can start to think strategically about how to achieve them. There are four overlapping elements:

1. Acquiring a wide range of information about global trends in human behavior, technology, and business in your field

2. Stopping to reflect in light of the new information and letting ideas "percolate"

3. Synthesizing the information into a creative vision of the future

4. Communicating the vision in a clear and compelling form

Leaders need not only manage their own attention but also capture others' attention. An inspiring strategic vision does this. It attracts and aligns our energy, creating an energizing set of ideals and tapping into our needs, hopes, and dreams.[1]

In order to think strategically and begin to create a vision, Sally needed to make the MindShift from Task Analysis to Market Analysis. This involved shifting from solving micro problems such as how each store should display its products, to macro problems like what products were likely to do best the following season.

Task Analysis . . . . **Market Analysis**
Problem-solving the best way to   Deciding what business to be in, a vision
accomplish a task   for where it should go, and strategies to
                                                                           to get there

————————————————————————————————————→

Making this transition depended on her refocusing her attention from narrow to wide. She needed to open up her mind, leaving aside self-focused questions like "Can I complete this task?" and moving toward holistic business questions like "Should we be in this business?"

Sally also needed a wider focus of attention to make the MindShift from Personal Accountability for her own deadlines and goals to Organizational Accountability where she measured the performance of the organization as a whole.

Personal Accountability . . . . **Organizational Accountability**
Monitoring your own work processes,   Measuring the organization's success
deadlines and goals   (profit, efficiency, quality, service);
                                                          allocating and brokering resources

————————————————————————————————————→

These shifts were difficult for her because her ability to move quickly and get things done is what had made her successful on the smaller playing field of the European stores. As a leader at the next level she had to let go of doing and embrace thinking.

Sally suffered from the common misconception that it was her job alone to create her organization's vision. It freed her up to realize that pushing and selling her own vision would only create passivity. Instead, her role was to bring together her team members' individual visions. Sally organized a process to do this and was able to mobilize a great deal of energy in her employees. As a naturally extroverted and intuitive leader, she was able to excite each person about the task of identifying their unique purpose and connecting it to a shared organizational vision.

> One of the chief imperatives of leadership is to have vision. Vision requires a deep understanding of your business and is inspired by out-of-the-box thinking and imagination. Leaders need to make the time to reflect in peace to let their vision come together.
> — *Management Board Member,*
> *Fortune 50 Financial Services Company*

As a final step, you need to bring your vision down to earth and make it concrete. **If no one knows what the vision means in terms of what they are supposed to do, it is worthless.** JFK's "Put a man on the moon by the end of the decade," concretizes a vision in a concise, actionable statement. Once your organization has articulated its vision, each team then needs to translate it into a local version that specifies tangible objectives and milestones.

Sally's organization created a vision of bringing cutting-edge fashion to the market at a price every American could afford. This connected to Sally's purpose of helping people express their creativity and feel good about themselves. In addition, the vision of affordable fashion served as a guide for the design and merchandising teams in creating new products. They knew how to get behind it and bring it to life.

Another client of mine, Brad, took a different approach given the challenges he faced after taking on a new role in a company under siege. Brad had joined one of the largest banks in the world in the midst of its worst crisis ever. The markets had put it in a very difficult position, necessitating financial assistance from the U.S. government. The head of the institutional business, Kevin, had recruited Brad to head up human resources. Poised and thoughtful, Brad was a consummate professional. He brought a wealth of experience, and his maturity and composure were tremendous assets given the uncertainty and anxiety in the business.

Brad realized he needed a clear talent strategy to help the organization get through the storm. Competitors were trying to pick off his best talent, and high potentials were unsure of their prospects. Brad understood his line clients were too preoccupied to engage in a long blank-slate visioning exercise. He decided to combine top-down and bottom-up approaches starting with his HR team.

He asked his direct reports to begin talking to their teams about what they felt were the most important initiatives going forward. Then he brought his team together and got them to craft a consensus vision. Finally, he engaged each of the seven business unit heads to refine the plan and ensure it aligned with how they saw their talent needs changing over the next two or three years.

The outcome was a concise set of strategic imperatives that energized Brad's HR team and focused the business heads on what they needed to do. Wayne, Brad's head of leadership development, facilitated a series of rigorous talent reviews. Each business leader had to know who was their top talent, how to invest in them, and how to retain them. Rather than being a one-off event, talent updates are now part of each quarterly business review to ensure focus and follow up. In addition, campus recruiting got renewed attention as a means to bring in the best new talent and build toward the future. Senior executives visited elite schools across the world to encourage graduates to consider the bank as a place where they could have greater responsibility and challenges than other firms.

Kevin understood Brad's strategy and put his energy behind it. He made a number of concrete and symbolic moves that highlighted its importance. Kevin recognized the hard-working recruiter team with a special bonus, which was a welcome surprise given the economic environment. He also personally called the best interns to invite them to join the bank at the end of the summer. Brad's strategy not only helped his business get through the storm, but as the economy turned around, it was poised to take advantage and leverage the foundation his team had helped build.

Chapter 10

Innovative Thinking

The computer was a game-changer. The Internet is still a game-changer. What will be the next game-changer? Innovation creates value beyond what is already here. It also transforms the rules of businesses.

The first stage of a new product's life is where the greatest percentage of revenue, profit, and market share is captured.[1] Once fast followers copy what is unique, they end the monopoly of the innovator and drive down costs. Ultimately, the product becomes a commodity, margins are compressed, and quality suffers. Many countries care little about protecting copyrights or intellectual property, which makes innovating quickly even more critical.

While innovation drives business, the mantra of many organizations today is, "Buy smaller and weaker companies with ideas, cut out infrastructure costs and increase efficiencies." While we need to do things better and more efficiently, we can do better than at that. **We need to do things differently.**

Simon was the SVP of mail services in a Fortune 50 company. He had several thousand employees on his team across the world. Having worked his way up the ranks for thirty years, he knew all the ins and outs of his department. He had seen it all and was suspicious of anything new. I started coaching him when he was fifty-nine years old and looking forward to retiring in a couple of years. His function was performing adequately, and his 360 reviews were largely positive. His boss, however, expected more. He expected improved processes, better service, cost savings, and a vision that would motivate people to achieve stretch objectives. Simon's reaction to all this was "Ugh."

Changing perspective is at the heart of mindful learning as well as creative problem-solving.[2] Every time we hear a business situation we can choose to frame it as a problem or a challenge. Simon was able to get behind his initial "Ugh" reaction and start to see the possibilities for change. He actively experimented with different perspectives to understand potential new strategies. Shifting his perspective in this way depended on his learning to manage his attention. This ultimately enabled him to start reflecting on the rules of the game he was playing.

The customer's perspective is the most important one to adopt for innovative thinking because all new products and services are driven by human needs in search of a better solution. Knowing your customers' needs and concerns at a visceral level results in the best service and the best innovations. Online social networking communities are not a substitute for in-person relationships. However, they can connect employees and customers in order to have a conversation about their perspectives and needs.

Experiment: Creative Problem-Solving Using Perspective Taking

Think of a complex situation you are facing.

1. Consider two possible frames. First, think about the situation as a problem. Then, frame it as a challenge. Consider how this changes your attitude and how you think and feel about the situation.

2. Adopt the perspective of a customer with unlimited resources and ask yourself what you would do. Warren Buffett would not wait on hold for a customer service representative to take his call. He would have his assistant get him when the call went through.

3. Automate the solution to make it cost-effective. We don't have unlimited resources, but the Warren Buffett solution suggests an idea. Why don't more companies automatically call us back when they are free instead of making us wait? This would save them toll charges and our untold frustration.

4. Look at your situation upside down. In other words, look at any symmetries involved and reverse them so you are looking at them backward. The upside down ketchup bottle uses this principle.

Priceline is another example of using symmetry. Why not have customers set prices instead of vendors?

5. Change your channel (e.g., draw a picture of the problem, listen to music, get up and move).

◆ ◆ ◆

We can learn a great deal about creativity and learning from children. For them everything is new and potentially wonderful (they naturally demonstrate beginner's mind). Moreover, children accelerate their learning by playing. They don't just play to win, they love to make up new rules and new games. The essence of play is the engagement of imagination, and it has a remarkable ability to focus the mind and promote discovery.[3] Play creates both learning and the experience of joy, and on a physical level stimulates neural development and connectivity.[4] The ping pong tables and game rooms in technology and marketing companies are not just feel-good retention tools. They help us break our thinking patterns and foster cultures that are more likely to give birth to innovation.

Stepping back to listen to one's customers and reflect on their feedback is critical. Executives like to think they are customer-centric, but risk falling out of touch. In our online communities, customers not only give us feedback and insight, they share a lot about their lives from daily minutia to their overarching frustrations and dreams. When you go further and ask them to help you innovate, it not only gives you ideas you would never have thought of, it builds incredible brand loyalty and enthusiasm.

—*Diane Hessan, President and CEO, Communispace*

One of the best predictors of creativity is self-perception. If you think of yourself as creative you are more likely to be creative.[5] Everyone can create, and your own self-limiting assumptions are the biggest obstacle.[6] I cringed when I heard Simon say he was not creative. I often hear this from executives who have worked for years in technical or operational roles. They have given up on themselves in terms of creative ability and were probably told early on that, because they were not artistic, they were not creative. It is never too late to undo such lessons.

Self-limiting assumptions are also an obstacle whenever we hear an idea and respond, "We tried that and it failed." While we need to be aware of realistic constraints, focusing on these too early in problem-solving can squelch creative energy and undermine confidence. Simon was initially pessimistic about change. He had been in his function so long that he thought he knew what worked and what didn't. He was loathe to waste time and money on experiments. He began to build back his confidence by practicing taking small risks with his team and suspending judgment until they objectively evaluated the outcomes. This is part of the magic of the technique of brainstorming. Our critical, negative habit is so strong that we need to set aside a time when all ideas can be put on the table. Simon encouraged his team to brainstorm and play with new ideas. He restrained himself from commenting prematurely as he had seen a number of the ideas they initially came up with fail in the past.

In addition to challenging negative thinking, a powerful way to overcome self-limiting assumptions is self-hypnosis. Self-hypnosis puts your conscious mind into a trance in order to tap the power of your unconscious. Self-hypnosis has proven to be one of the most effective ways of changing habitual behavior (e.g., weight loss, smoking cessation) as well as improving performance in stressful situations (e.g., Olympic competition, public speaking). Self-hypnosis opens your mind and frees you from the self-conscious worry, cognitive filtering, and negative assumptions that interfere with learning and performance. It is excellent for cultivating creativity, examining alternative perspectives, and helping leaders clarify their vision.

In thirty years as an operations manager, Simon was never expected to have a vision. Rather, he got things done by making lists. He would carefully prioritize each issue that came up and get a great deal of satisfaction from ticking them off one by one. However, he thrived on challenge, and told me, "What the hell, what have I got to lose at this point in my life?" Though initially skeptical, he let me teach him self-hypnosis and dutifully practiced several times a week. His wife thought he had gone mad.

Innovation is as much a product of the environments we create as the people within them.[7] Simon looked for ways to help his people be creative by fostering greater autonomy, structuring challenging assignments, ensuring available resources, and encouraging mutual support from colleagues. Simon also needed to anticipate the resistance that new ideas and ways of working create — no one likes disruption and uncertainty. Simon understood that thinking more independently didn't mean he should operate independently. Early on he enlisted the most open-minded member of his team as an ally. Laura had a great deal of potential and Simon thought she could possibly be his successor. With Laura's help he planned how to introduce changes gradually so they could be embraced by as many of his team as possible.

Innovation is about learning to take calculated risks. However, executives cite their own risk-averse cultures as the most significant reason for their failure to realize returns on innovation initiatives.[8] As in many publicly held companies, the short-term focus on quarterly results in Simon's organization had left little energy for recruiting innovative thinkers, rewarding greater risk-taking and investing in new technology. Many of Simon's direct reports had been in the organization more than twenty years, and so were initially as attached to the status quo as he was. Simon got his people to ask themselves what the worst thing was that could happen. Besides losing the security of the known, were they afraid of failure, looking foolish, or being criticized? Taking calculated risks meant examining these potential downsides by comparing them to the risk of not acting. He was able to get his people to see that not acting could mean the entire function could be outsourced. While many of his team were close to retirement themselves, none of them wanted this to be their legacy.

Self-hypnosis enabled Simon to approach his work in a completely different way. Rather than always "efforting" (doggedly going after each item on his list) he could experiment with "allowing" (patiently letting his unconscious solve problems). Simon cultivated a more receptive attention and gradually began to let go of his obsessive list-making. He became more fluid in his operating and management style. He became more creative and started to value creativity more in others. Rather than having to generate every new idea himself, he was able to listen to his people's ideas and select the ones with most potential and nurture them. He engaged his team in creating a vision for the future that was inspiring and that they could continue to implement without him when he retired.

Self-hypnosis also enabled Simon to open his mind about how he could use his skills during retirement. Having worked twelve-hour days for years, he was scared of what his future would look like and knew he could not be satisfied playing tennis every day. He was able to network and find volunteer opportunities where he could mentor people early in their careers. Having coached Laura intensively for the last two years of his tenure, he was able to pass the reins to her, and he made a smooth transition out of his role. His wife now calls him a new man (which gives him a chuckle) and neither of them can believe the changes he has made.

Experiment: Self-Hypnosis

Use the guidelines below to put yourself in trance. You can memorize the instructions, or even better, read them into a tape recorder. Your own voice is more powerful than anyone's for inducing a hypnotic state.

Self-hypnosis and meditation both use a state of relaxation as their starting points. However, in self-hypnosis you put your conscious mind to sleep, whereas during meditation you are trying to "fall awake." As with any skill, you will get better with practice and soon be able to quickly put yourself in a light trance. You can do this right before any event where you need to be optimally focused without being tense. For example, going into a light trance before giving a presentation, going on an interview, or hitting a golf ball can significantly improve your performance.

Guidelines for Self-Hypnosis

1. Start any time you feel irritable, frustrated, or blocked. Place your hands in a comfortable spot on your body (use the same place each time to serve as an "anchor"). Allow your eyelids to gently close and turn your attention inward.

2. Focus your attention on your breathing; count five breaths; now focus on your hands; feel your fingers becoming warm.

3. Turn your attention to inner experiences of: relaxation, comfort, warmth, heaviness (or lightness), peacefulness, radiance (or pick your own quality). Allow these feelings to spread and amplify.

4. Scan down your body, allowing each muscle to relax and coming back to your breathing every so often. Feel your body softening, muscles releasing and boundaries dissolving. Scan down again, noticing how you can relax still further. Feel a wave of relaxation spreading down your body, cleansing your cells and emptying toxins out holes you imagine in the bottoms of your feet. Explore any and all subtle sensations that come up in your body (e.g., tingling, vibration or pulsing).

5. Picture yourself in a favorite place. Include as many elements as possible in your image, including tactile (e.g., a breeze on your cheek or the warmth of the sun on your skin) and auditory sensations (e.g., the sound of waves or water flowing in a stream).

6. Begin to *wonder* how your conscious mind can let go further and further, and how your unconscious can do whatever it needs for your healing. For example:

   a. allowing your muscles to remain relaxed at work

   b. maintaining perspective during conflicts

   c. examining and letting go of fears and anxieties wherever they come up

   d. undoing and releasing yourself from negative thinking

   e. exploring and developing your capacity for problem-solving using your previous life experiences

   f. moving beyond learned limitations and limited definitions of yourself

7. Remind yourself that what you have learned will always be readily available. Affirm that practicing regularly will enable you to go into trance more quickly, effortlessly, and completely and resolve to continue practicing. Repeat any other affirmations you want to reinforce to support your growth.

8. Allow yourself ten or twenty minutes before returning to a fully conscious waking state. When you feel ready, gradually bring yourself back — feeling awake, energized and refreshed. Count back from three to one, slowly letting your eyes float open.

◆ ◆ ◆

Visualization is a form of self-hypnosis. Both require you to relax your body and go into an altered state of consciousness to be effective. Athletes and artists have used positive visualization for many years to increase performance. By imagining how they will act to get the desired outcome they are able to practice without risk of injury and increase both their confidence and chances of success. Positive visualization also works for a wide range of emotional and physical ailments. One of the first advocates of positive visualization was Dr. Bernie Segal, who showed that it could facilitate cancer treatment.

Visualizing successful performance is most effective when we combine a visual image with as many other sensory experiences as possible (e.g., tactile and auditory sensations). It is also important to add whatever visceral feeling is associated with success. If performing well goes with a tingling in your shoulders and stomach, then add that to your visualization.

When you visualize in this way you are practicing the process that leads to successful outcomes and focusing less on visualizing the successful outcome. You can get as much as two-thirds of the same effect as actual practice by visualizing successful process.[9] This kind of mental rehearsal trains your attention to evoke identical physiological states as actual performance and strengthens the neural connections you need to perform new behavior fluidly.[10]

If you would like to try self-hypnosis or visualization and would rather not make your own tape, Belleruth Naparstek has created a comprehensive set of recordings (*www.healthjourneys.com*).

Chapter 11

Stress Management
and Resilience

I first was introduced to high levels of stress during final exams at Yale. Each semester ended with a week of difficult back-to-back exams, which could mean the difference between passing and failing. I think exams are great at measuring recall, but lousy at evaluating a whole semester's worth of learning. Finals week did, however, teach me about my coping skills. As grueling as the week was, it was soon over, and I learned I could survive the intense stress. The short-term challenge of solving difficult problems can actually be healthy. Like exercise, periodic stress can make us stronger and more resilient.

When you have few challenges in your work, you do not learn much or perform very well. Think of a job or time in your career when you were coasting. Perhaps you avoided tasks that were outside your comfort zone, and you traded off being secure for being a little bored. On the other hand, too much stress in not healthy either. Think of a job or assignment that stretched you beyond your abilities. You may have started worrying about being criticized for mistakes, and at times your body would tense up and your attention would freeze. Extreme stress like this can cause primitive centers in your brain to be activated and for you to revert to instinctual, survival behaviors like the "fight or flight" response.[1] In these situations you are less able to use your higher logical brain (the cortex), and your flexibility and performance go down. When you are too worried about failing, you become reluctant to experiment with new behaviors, and thus less able to learn.

The diagram on the following page shows this relationship between stress and learning & performance. When stress is too low, learning and performance are also low. When stress is too high, learning and

69

STRESS/PERFORMANCE RELATIONSHIP

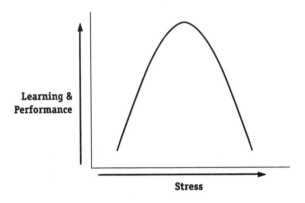

performance are similarly suppressed. The goal is to be able to monitor how much stress you are under and your ability to manage it, so you know where you are on the curve and can perform at your peak.

I got introduced to chronic stress as a doctoral student in clinical psychology at New York University. The courses introduced complex psychodynamic and statistical theory, and there was a great deal of assigned reading every week. I had to teach during the semesters and take part-time jobs to earn a living. I also started seeing patients in the clinic and getting supervised on this work. I thoroughly enjoyed learning from each activity, but there was just too much at once, and the juggling never seemed to stop. To top it all off, there was THE DISSERTATION. I had never taken on a project of that magnitude, and it took everything I had to complete it.

As I lived this chronic stress I started studying all of its negative effects and wondering what illnesses I would come down with next. Chronic stress can lead to cancer, diabetes, heart disease, and allergies by creating inflammation that wears down your immune system.[2] In fact, as many as 90 percent of the complaints seen by physicians seem to be stress-related.[3] Stress also contributes to the development of mental illnesses, including anxiety, depression, schizophrenia, and personality disorders.

The academic literature on stress offered me little practical help, so I sought out additional training and was introduced to mindfulness. As I mentioned earlier, mindfulness training has a number of positive impacts on physical and mental functioning. Beyond reducing stress and anxiety, it has been shown to alleviate hypertension, arthritis, insomnia, inflammation, cancer, depression, and infertility.[4] The research convinced me of its value. I began to practice regular meditation, and this proved incredibly helpful in surviving graduate school.

My experience with meditation made me curious about how mindfulness works, and I was led to the stress hormone cortisol. Cortisol is released by your adrenal glands in order to mobilize your body to face challenge, but it can cause your organs to break down when they are exposed to it chronically. In addition, cortisol interferes with learning, critical thinking and creativity.[5] Interestingly, cortisol is released not only under stress, but also during thrill-seeking and high-stimulation activities.[6] Thus, bungee jumping and racing a car down a highway can cloud your judgment, as can simply overloading yourself by taking on too much at once.

Swedish researcher Marianne Frankenhaeuser measured cortisol in employees at the top and bottom of a number of large organizations.[7] She found that stress and high levels of cortisol are associated with the experience of helplessness and lack of control, all of which are more common in individuals at the bottom of the totem pole. Senior executives also experience high levels of stress, but this appears to be moderated by the higher degree of control they have over their environments.

One way that meditation appears to work is by reducing cortisol levels in your blood.[8] Mindfulness also increases the feedback you get from your body and thus helps you know how to take care of yourself. In other words, it helps you know where you are on the stress/performance curve. When you listen to your body and tune in to its signals, you know where to give yourself attention and what to do. This includes making sure you take care of fundamentals, like proper exercise, diet, and sleep.

It can be useful to think of yourself as an athlete and to design your self-care regimen with the same discipline.[9] One of my clients, Dan, concluded that he was on a continual sprint. He was devoted to his wife and two boys and realized that if he wanted to ensure his personal and professional longevity, he needed to think more like a marathon runner. Dan had plenty of intense challenge at work so boredom was never the

SOURCES OF STRESS

External   **Internal**

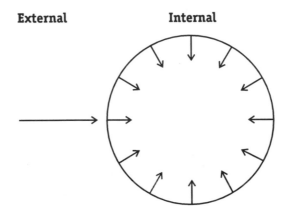

issue. Rather, he was at risk of burning out and was starting to experience chest pains. He began going home earlier and building in time in the evenings and on weekends for rest, recovery, and "not doing." Dan made a commitment to other positive habits like mindful breathing and regular exercise. His regimen ensured he had the energy and endurance necessary to succeed in his high-pressure job. More importantly, he is still alive and enjoying raising his sons.

In addition to the physical and external sources of stress, a large component of stress is psychological (or internal). As the ancient Greek Epictetus declared in A.D. 85, stress is caused by how you think about events, not the events themselves.[10] As in the earlier example of losing a job, if you believe you do not have the skills to find a new job (such as networking and interviewing), you will feel threatened and experience stress. On the other hand, if you believe you have marketable skills and some potentially interesting career paths, you will feel positive challenge.

While it can provide some momentary relief to complain about all the things that are causing you stress from outside, you typically can't do much about these (the large arrow in the diagram). **The bulk of your stress comes from within you** (the internal arrows). In addition, the stress you create for yourself is the only stress you really have control over and thus it is the best place to intervene.

Experiment: Identifying Sources of Stress

The first step in managing stress is to become aware of its sources and triggers. Make a list of all the sources of stress in your life. Once you have done this, see if the items fall into these categories:

- Goal stress: frustration from things getting in your way
- Rule stress: anger when others break your imposed "shoulds" and "musts"
- Identity stress: confusion from not knowing who you are
- Time and volume stress: when you take on too much
- Fear stress: worry about potential loss — real or imagined
- Sensory stress: from illness, pain, or injury
- Change stress: from role or job changes, or moving your home/family
- Loss stress: losing an important relationship or family member

Having identified some of the sources of your stress, are there any small changes you could make in your life to reduce it? Are there sources of external stress that are outside of your control and not going away, and thus you can stop spending energy on? Some sources of stress (e.g., fear and identity stress) are anything but quick fixes. Having a professional coach, counselor, or therapist for these can be especially helpful.

◆ ◆ ◆

Being a perfectionist and interested in stress, I decided to study how perfectionists handle failure for my doctoral thesis. I gave subjects a test to measure their perfectionist attitudes. Then I had them take an intelligence test that they were told most people pass. I rigged the test so everyone failed. (I know, it was a little sadistic, but I screened out anyone who was clinically depressed before giving the test.) After the test I sent the subjects home. The next day they came back to the lab and I assessed how they felt and what they had thought about overnight.

Perhaps not surprisingly, subjects who had more perfectionist attitudes were more depressed the next day.[11] More interesting was that they reported more self-critical thoughts and rumination overnight. While a number of theories had suggested that self-critical thinking leads people to feel worse about themselves,[12] no one had demonstrated this effect over time.

To know if our thinking is distorted and causing us stress we need to be able to maintain perspective and objectively reflect on it. Does it really make sense for me to beat myself up because I failed an intelligence test? In the case of Keith (the black belt graphic artist), does it really need to threaten my professional identity if a colleague criticizes my work? In order to assess the rationality of our thinking we first must become aware of it, which is where mindfulness comes in.

When we turn mindful attention to our thinking, we become aware that there is a great deal of mental chatter just below the level of awareness. These "automatic thoughts" are often irrational and self-critical. Gently challenging them and replacing them with more rational and positive alternatives is a central strategy in managing stress.

Like Keith, most of my clients are Type As. They are overachievers who are driven to prove themselves and their value, which is part of what has made them successful. However, many of these executives have experienced only success in their careers and do not know how to deal with criticism or failure when it comes. We all instinctively get defensive and blame other people when things go wrong. However, this response cuts off learning, and in the extreme, can result in executive "derailment" (i.e., being fired). The most successful executives are able to maintain high standards without becoming perfectionists and can understand the concept of healthy failure. They are able to reframe what might appear from the outside as failure more adaptively, considering it feedback and an opportunity to learn.[13]

Experiment: Building a Stress Management Plan Using Mindful Intelligence

There are so many potential sources of stress that it is difficult to separate stress management from other leadership skills. For example, miscommunications can be a large source of stress, and so communication skills are important. Similarly, building strong relationships are key to increasing social support, which is another central ingredient in managing stress.

The most important ways to work with stress fall into six categories of Mindful Intelligence — Mindful, Physical, Emotional, Social, Spiritual, and Cognitive. By applying mindfulness broadly we are able to build our intelligence in each category. Pick two or three strategies that resonate for you from each of the categories (like making your own dish on a Chinese menu). Commit to exploring and practicing these as part of your development plan. Some of the techniques will be discussed more fully in subsequent chapters.

◆ ◆ ◆

MINDFUL INTELLIGENCE STRATEGIES

Mindful Intelligence — Cultivating present-focused, open, and accepting attention to increase self-awareness

- Identify buttons, triggers, and symptoms
- Be aware of holding and controlling your breathing
- Heed the messages of your body and emotions and look into their sources
- Challenge your thinking and beliefs; practice non-judging
- Be mindful of your consumption — eating, drinking, self-medicating, buying, and suffering from media and information overload
- Regularly slow down and stop doing; be and attend without intending
- Learn self-hypnosis/visualization to leverage your unconscious

Physical Intelligence — Taking care of yourself

- Distinguish self-care from selfishness and self-indulgence
- Understand your impact on your environment; spend time in and care for nature to reset your attention
- Understand your environment's impact on you; design and organize your work setting
- Establish healthy habits, especially diet, exercise and sleep; also consider stretching, Yoga, Tai Chi, and massage

- Use rituals and positive, self-reinforcing routines to develop self-discipline
- Simplify, let go, and set limits; beware of over-tolerance and over-commitment

Emotional Intelligence — Learning to use feelings productively and to be positive and resilient

- Check your attitude; reframe problems as challenges
- Explore and confront fears
- Develop self-acceptance; appreciate both your strengths and vulnerabilities
- Avoid the self-criticism/self-esteem trap (I will feel good if...)
- Come back to what you want; be aware of "musts" and "shoulds"
- Examine your expectations and assumptions; beware of personalizing
- Take time outs to stop, reflect, and avoid emotional hijacking; circle back to difficult problems or conflicts when you are ready
- Have fun, play, and find reasons to laugh

Social Intelligence — Giving and getting support by building lasting, intimate relationships

- Practice Mindful Dialogue: deep listening and focused speech
- Learn to negotiate win/win; tune in to others' goals, needs, and concerns
- Don't protect others from their feelings or take responsibility for their dramas
- Express yourself: emotionally and creatively
- Offer service to others: giving is receiving
- Create a personal board of directors with sounding boards, mentors, sponsors, counselors, and coaches
- Build a strong network and a community that supports your development

Spiritual Intelligence — Finding meaning and purpose outside materialism

- Explore and define your values
- Practice forgiveness; explore and let go of anger
- Remind yourself what you can be grateful for
- Where you do not have much control, think about where you still have choices
- Focus on process vs. outcomes
- Don't chase happiness and accept what is; be patient with yourself and your development
- Trust your feelings, intuitions, and life
- Keep perspective; ask, "Does this really matter?" and "What are the real consequences?"

Cognitive Intelligence — Planning, problem-solving, and committing

- Write down your vision, goals, and actions and communicate them
- Take responsibility for how you manage yourself and your time
- Anticipate obstacles; plan rather than worry
- Cultivate flexible thinking; beware of black/white, absolute, and negative thinking
- Practice new behavior; work from the outside in by acting "as if" you are confident and composed
- Solicit ongoing feedback; monitor progress and reward positive momentum

I love teaching stress management and resilience workshops. By just doing a few things differently, people can see the immediate impact on their quality of life. Moreover, the topic allows people from widely different backgrounds to open up, become vulnerable with each other, and connect very quickly. In one workshop at an Internet company, a senior executive sat next to a man who worked in the mailroom. Though the causes of their stress were different, their experience and challenges were very similar, which allowed them to learn from each other. A month after the workshop I hold a follow-up session to problem-solve any obstacles, review skills, and enable participants to support each others' momentum. Participants rate their resilience, comparing the four weeks before the first workshop with the four weeks since then. It is gratifying to see the dramatic changes people make, as shown in the graph.

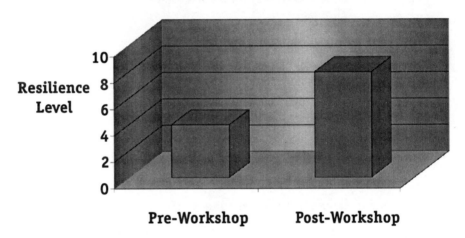

IMPACT OF RESILIENCE TRAINING

Chapter 12

Communication

Wendy (the executive from chapter 1) was a very fast thinker. She had so many ideas going on in her head that it was hard for her to be silent and listen. There was an urgency to her speech, as if she was worried that if she didn't say everything she was thinking her ideas would be lost. Wendy was like many smart executives who have minds like televisions they can't turn off. With so many signals and information going nonstop, their brain gets overheated, and they can have trouble shutting down. This makes it hard for them to be present with their families and at times hard for them to sleep.[1] Wendy first had to learn to quiet and tame her mind using mindfulness exercises. Then supporting techniques could keep her focused, like writing ideas down on a pad during meetings so she could think before sharing them.

The MindShift Wendy had to master was going from Exchanging Information to Communicating.

Exchanging Information . . . . Communicating
Giving and receiving information about your own activities
Creating a two-way dialogue with a wide constituent group about your organization's activities and your future plan, vision, and brand

As someone who had earned her stripes executing a large number of transactions as fast as possible, Wendy had to work hard to change her habits and make this shift.

As the leader of a large sales organization, Sabina also understood the tendency of her people to become transactional. In some situations simply exchanging information, trading, and closing deals is sufficient. However, she understood that if transacting became a substitute for connecting, her people could not build successful long-term client relationships. As a leader, she needed to model effectively creating a two-way dialogue with hundreds of people.

The true goal of communication is connection. The desire for connection comes from caring. If I am genuinely interested in who you are I will do more than listen passively; I will build off what I hear and go deeper into understanding who you are. Once we are connected and understand each other we can build the common ground and accountability needed to work as partners.   —*Sabina McCarthy, Senior Executive, Global Wealth Management Firm*

Communication shares the same root as "communion." Thus, at its core, communication is about connecting, sharing, and community. Effective communication is the foundation of organizations where employees have meaningful, mutually supportive relationships. Sabina's insight is that when employees truly care about one another, the positive feelings and morale not only sustain them through setbacks, but enable them to produce extraordinary business results.

Discussion and debate are the most common forms of communication. Here logic and willpower do battle and we hope the survivor of this "natural selection" is the best and strongest idea. In contrast, dialogue is a creative process where each party enters not knowing quite where the conversation will go. **Suspending our own biases and agendas and trusting in the dialogue process makes it possible for us to learn and create something new.**

Mindful dialogue is speaking and listening with careful attention. Deep listening requires us to quiet our internal dialogue and manage our needs for attention so they do not overtake the speaker's needs. Focused speaking requires us to know where we are going in advance and anticipate what will attract the listener's attention.

Communicating mindfully means attending to when we are listening and when we tune out, or as my friend Gregor Simon-MacDonald puts it, "listening to how we listen." It also means listening to our bodies and emotions and using this information as we are communicating.

Experiment: Mindful Dialogue

Read the mindful dialogue principles below and pick one principle from Deep Listening and one from Focused Speaking to practice in your conversations this week. Add other principles as you get more comfortable with each one.

MINDFUL DIALOGUE
Deep Listening

Preparation

- **Attitude Check** — are you really interested in listening, learning and connecting with this person in order to create something new? If not, don't fake it.

- **Preparation** — Take a few breaths and allow yourself to relax so you can focus your attention. Be quiet and still. Turn down your internal dialogue and listen against a background of silence.

- **Body Language** — Make eye contact, turn toward the speaker and position your body in a way that demonstrates your receptivity.

Self-Awareness

- **Be aware of how your own needs** (e.g., to feel appreciated or noticed) can distract you from going deeper into the speaker's experience. Be aware of:

  – Interrupting with your own reactions or stories.

  – Preparing responses and questions rather than listening.

  – Premature problem-solving.

- **Keep your mind as open as possible.** Be aware of prematurely judging or evaluating what you hear. Also be aware of agreeing/disagreeing or comparing what you believe with what is said.

- **Pay attention to the inner speaker,** not just the outer appearance. Focus on experiencing the world from the speaker's perspective and position rather than focusing on your own feelings and reactions.

The Message

- **Look for clues to underlying messages.** Use open-ended questions to draw out/tune in to hidden feelings, desires and concerns.

- Ask yourself if you understand the speaker's implicit message. Decide if you need to **paraphrase or validate** what you hear.

- **Decide what not to listen to.** Be aware of eavesdropping and taking in negative conversations and communications. Pay attention to what kind of information you choose to take in.

MINDFUL DIALOGUE
Focused Speaking

Preparation

- **Attitude check** — do you respect the other person; do you see him or her as a "means" or an "end"?

- **Preparation** — take a moment to think about your broader intent beyond conveying information. Anticipate how your message will be received and match your energy and positivity with the impact you want to have.

- **Body Language** — Check in with your breathing and posture. What feelings do your tone, body language and facial expression convey? Are they consistent with each other?

Self-Awareness

- Be aware of expecting or demanding attention. Invite attention and two-way conversations by speaking from present-focused experience:

  - Speak for yourself using "I" statements like "I want...I think... and I feel..."

  - Minimize distractions and tangents.

- Be aware of how and why you are talking about others without them present.

- Make sure examples are timely. Be careful about repeating old stories in "lecture" mode.

- Avoid clichés, technical language, jargon and words with private meanings.

The Message

• **Reduce ambiguities and contradictions** (e.g., "Yes, but...").

• **Streamline content** so you eliminate details and anything that is not necessary and purposeful.

• **Break each point into a manageable size.** Pause and take a breath between ideas.

• **Present the rationale/data behind your conclusions and invite critiques;** be ready to suspend and inquire into your assumptions.

• **Be aware of whether your listener is paying attention** and if you need to validate his or her understanding.

◆ ◆ ◆

Deep listening has three elements: preparation, self-awareness, and message. Start preparing for a conversation you have coming up by thinking about your goal. Are you hoping to get something tangible or some information from the other person? If so, this is fine, but consider how transacting may limit what you can accomplish.

Preparation also involves assessing your readiness to listen. How often have you been interrupted by someone in the middle of an important project or thought and been reluctant to check if talking later would work for that person? If you decide this is actually an okay time, take a few breaths and allow yourself to relax so you can focus your attention before you try to listen. If you are in the middle of a thought, write it down so you are not preoccupied while you are listening.

When I teach mindful dialogue I break the group into pairs so one person is the speaker while the other person listens. In the first speaker/listener exercise the job of the listener is simply to stay silent and listen. I call time and give everyone five minutes. After just three or four minutes the whole room is usually buzzing with speakers and listeners going back and forth, everyone excitedly interrupting with their own stories and problem-solving rather than listening. I call time-out and we talk about what happened. Increasing your self-awareness as a listener depends on becoming sensitive to your needs and managing your internal distractions. It is challenging to continually refocus on the speaker as your own reactions, ideas, and experiences come up and you want to share them. After one or two more rounds the group is usually able to settle, and people experience how refreshing it is to really be listened to.

Experiment: Listening with Beginner's Mind

Go to YouTube and listen for a few minutes to a politician you don't know. Try to listen to how you listen. Come back to reading after you have done this.

If you have even a slight political leaning toward left or right, the minute an idea appears to match your own beliefs, you may find yourself judging all is good and stop listening for anything new. If what you hear does not agree with what you believe, you may find yourself judging it to be a poor idea, reject it, and again stop listening. Studies show we more easily spot inconsistency in an opposing candidate's message and ignore our own candidate's hypocrisy.[2] Our brains appear to be wired for consistency. Inconsistency with our values is distracting, and so we screen out information that disagrees with what we believe. Unfortunately, this makes it harder to learn or change our minds.

Listening with beginner's mind means suspending our constant evaluation reflex so that we can take in an idea before deciding what to do with it. Listening in this way enables us to get closer to the "inner speaker," experiencing how others see the world from their vantage point.[3]

◆ ◆ ◆

Listening deeply means trying to understand the multiple levels of meaning in a communication. The first part of the message is the actual words used and their grammatical interpretation. Next is what the speakers are thinking as they speak and the feelings they are conveying with their words. The last level is the speaker's intention or request.

A couple of weeks ago I got home and my wife, Lisa, said, "Your father called, call him back right away." Her words were relatively clear. However, underneath I wasn't sure. Her feeling might be frustration or concern, and her thinking might be that I should call because I created some issue, or I am the best person to call because I have a good relationship with my father. Lisa's intention could be that I should solve some problem.

To know whether any of these interpretations was correct required me to be more active as a listener. I needed to pay attention to all the available verbal and nonverbal cues, including using my gut feelings and intuition. One of the best ways I have found to do this is to use the physical sensations in my body as a guide. If I tense up when I hear concern in Lisa's voice, I guess there is trouble. Sensing some underlying message, I draw her out by asking open-ended questions (questions that demonstrate I do not already have an answer in mind). I learn that my father was having trouble breathing today and so my mom took him to the doctor. I was right about there being trouble, and now I am more worried. At this point validating and paraphrasing what I heard helps me to test my understanding before I do anything. I ask a few more questions to find out how serious it is, and apparently the doctor said he is fine. He just needed to adjust his asthma medication. I begin to relax and take a few minutes to breathe. Now I can call my father with a clearer picture of what happened and in a better frame of mind to support him rather than dealing with my own anxiety when I call.

Deep listening does not mean listening to everyone and everything deeply. With all of the information that bombards us each day (emails, advertisements, the Internet), we need to set limits and choose what information we want to take in. We also need to be aware of the seductiveness of eavesdropping, gossiping, and joining "pity parties." The negativity of these interactions can easily drag us down. Being a mindful listener means being a mindful consumer of information.

Several years ago I tried to teach the principles of deep listening and focused speaking to a former Russian tank commander. Rod was the head of engineering in a software technology firm. He was a brilliant architect and had created one of the firm's most successful products. He ruled his team with fear, though they also respected him for his intellect. He was intensely competitive, let little get in his way, and had fierce debating skills. In his mind he was always right, and so he felt justified in simply pushing harder when he met any kind of opposition. The CEO and Rod's peers were fed up.

Rod was seldom direct, but it was always clear he had an agenda. He spoke to you only when he wanted to influence your thinking or get you to do something. However, he rarely anticipated the impact of this attitude, nor did he think about the messages his tone and body language sent. Coming into every interaction with fixed ideas in mind, he conveyed that where you were headed was wrong and he was there to save you. You got the message that he was superior and saw you as simply a means to an end. As a result, he quickly created resistance and resentment. He was stuck fighting battles and transacting. Connecting was out of the question. His peers described him as the most obnoxious and condescending person they had ever met.

It took me four months to get him to listen. It just didn't make sense to him because he already knew the right answers for everything. It finally clicked that listening was the only way he was going to get his ideas heard, and the only way to avoid having his peers try to thwart his every move. Then we turned to focused speaking. He had to work very hard to stay open to where other people wanted to take conversations and to treat them as equals. He practiced presenting the rationale and data behind his conclusions and inviting critiques. Starting to suspend and inquire into his assumptions took another two months.

Rod had a vision for the next generation of software, but he needed to get the board to back him because it required a major investment. In two weeks he had the opportunity to make a thirty-minute presentation to the board, and so we worked on preparing his message. He had never really cared about his audience. I had him research the backgrounds of each board member to create a picture of their positions, needs, and concerns. He then developed talking points and a set of headline reminders on index cards so he could stay on point. He made two or three slides to bring his ideas to life, but we decided to avoid a long PowerPoint deck so the board would stay focused on him rather than the screen.

Rod rehearsed what he was going to say and videotaped himself to ensure clarity and consistency. As we played back the video, I had him put himself in the board's shoes so he could edit his message and reduce unnecessary details and ambiguities. At the same time as he focused on preparation, Rod also needed to stay aware in the moment so he could invite and keep the board's attention. As cerebral as he was, it was vital he tap into his passion and feelings. If he lapsed into lecturing or technical jargon he would distance and lose them. He decided to tell the board a story of the future, using one of the firm's best customers as an example and showing how the new software would transform the customer's business.

Most talks end with a "Q&A" period, which is often an unfortunate sleeper. Rod carefully tracked the board's attention, and paused at times to validate their understanding rather than waiting till the end to see if they were still with him. The next day the CEO told him he had captured the board's imagination and he had the green light. Now all he had to do was get his peers to support him — the same peers that thought he was an obnoxious jerk.

Experiment: Speaker/Listener

Find a partner with whom you want to strengthen your relationship. This experiment is particularly good for spouses and close colleagues.[4] Start by finding a time and place where you can be focused and unhurried. Plan at least thirty minutes for the Silent Warm Up[5] and parts 1 and 2. Plan an additional thirty minutes for part 3.

Silent Warm Up

1. Close your eyes and take a few mindful breaths

2. Make the intention to be aware of and accept the other person

3. Now open your eyes, remaining silent for about thirty seconds

4. Close your eyes and silently process what you experienced

5. Open your eyes and experience both of you being here, receiving each other

6. Close your eyes and process the experience

7. Open your eyes and share your experiences with each other

Part 1: Listening for Content

Decide who will start as the speaker. Speakers talk for five minutes about any topic he wants, but saving heavy or emotional topics for part 2. Listeners *silently* attend to the content, and when the speaker is done, reflect back the content in maximum detail. Afterward the speaker clarifies what was accurate and what was missed. Speaker and listener then switch roles. This exercise is deceptively simple: the experience of listening and being listened to with this level of focus can be moving.

Part 2: Listening for Underlying Messages

For five minutes the speaker describes any topic they want, but preferably for this experiment something important. The listener pays attention to the underlying messages expressed. These include feelings (concerns, desires, mood) and intentions/attitudes (persuading, looking for sympathy, controlling, holding back). Here the listener tries to pay more attention to the nonverbal communication (tone of voice and body language). When the speaker is done, the listener reports what underlying feelings and messages they heard. The speaker clarifies what is on target and what was missed. Speaker and listener then switch roles. Getting out of our heads and into our bodies in this exercise allows speaker and listener to experience a deeper connection.

Part 3: Sharing Crucibles

Crucibles are pivotal times in our lives where we face significant stress. These periods force us to reexamine our values and make major life choices.[6] Speakers take ten minutes to describe a crucible, making sure to reflect on any values that the crucible reinforced for them. Listeners pay attention silently and afterward communicate the emotional impact of the story. Speaker and listener then switch roles. This experiment can connect even perfect strangers very quickly and be highly energizing as speaker and listener recommit to their values.

◆ ◆ ◆

Chapter 13

Emotional Intelligence

After six months of working with Rod I was ready to throw in the towel. In addition to being stubbornly attached to his agenda, he seemed emotionally tone deaf. He did not appear to care about people or what they felt about him. I do not like giving up on clients, but I felt I had to tell Rod and his boss that continuing coaching was not a good use of their time or money.

Just as I was getting ready to quit, Rod's successful presentation to the board renewed my optimism. He proved that he could learn by focusing on specific cues if he was motivated. The challenge of engaging his peers, though, was daunting. He was smart. His IQ was not the problem. He just had little emotional intelligence.

Emotional intelligence (or EI) is the ability to use the information in emotions to make decisions and reach goals.[1] Because leadership involves working through others, it is not surprising that EI is more predictive of leadership success than IQ or personality characteristics.[2] The essential components of EI are:[3]

* Reading and managing your emotions
* Understanding others' emotional signals
* Using emotions to help build relationships and reach goals

These skills are tremendously important for leaders and underlie the MindShift from Self-Awareness to Interpersonal Awareness. Inter-personal awareness allows you to communicate, negotiate, and influence effectively, as well as build strong relationships and create effective teams.

Self-Awareness . . . . **Interpersonal Awareness**
Knowing the strengths and weaknesses   Managing your emotions and behaviors
of your style   and their impact on others

$\longrightarrow$

Rod had no use for emotions. He believed they undermined logical problem-solving and caused unnecessary conflicts. Being somewhat competitive and cerebral myself, I occasionally lapsed into debating with him. I cited research showing emotions give meaning to events, tell us about our needs, motivate us and focus our energy.[4] He had a counter-argument for everything. "Feelings are irrational, arbitrary, and ambiguous," he told me. Because he couldn't trust them, he learned to be stoic and suppress them.

Rod's training in the army and as an engineer made it easy for him to buy into the corporate myth that emotions are dangerous and counter-productive and that you need to be tough to compete and survive. His dismissive attitude also served to cover his fear of feeling. He had watched enough people become overwhelmed by their feelings, and if starting to explore his feelings meant that, he wanted none of it. Many of my clients acknowledge intentionally staying distracted because of the fear of what they will feel if they stop moving. They continually distract themselves from feeling by diving into activity. Another strategy is to rationalize away feelings by telling ourselves it is not logical or reasonable to feel the way we do.

I had to agree with Rod that sometimes we have trouble letting go of feelings and overdramatize them. For example, we may feel we are betraying our prior organization after a takeover if we let go of sadness and anger too quickly and thus stay stuck. Or if we do not have the opportunity to fully express feelings of frustration, for example, because doing so impetuously with our boss could be career-limiting, we may bottle them up (repress them). This seldom works, and we often end up acting them out. Many people unconsciously fire themselves by demonstrating through their behavior that they are unhappy in their jobs. At some point their boss has to take them out of their misery to save the morale and productivity of the team.

The opposite of repressing feelings is venting them (e.g., pounding on a pillow or screaming). While this can provide some temporary relief, venting actually tends to strengthen negative emotions.[5] Venting overindulges negative feelings and reinforces the habit of not dealing with them. The alternative is to face, feel, name, and communicate feelings directly with words.

What Rod did not realize was that if we allow ourselves to fully experience our emotions we find they are inherently transient.[6] When we allow ourselves to hold them in our attention without judgment, they naturally dissolve and shift into another sensation. It is as if once we have heard their message, our emotions no longer need to call our attention. However, we still may need to make a decision or act on the information they give us.

What finally motivated Rod to explore the realm of feelings was his desire to save his marriage. His wife was fed up with his aloofness and poor listening. He had to start at the beginning, learning to recognize what he was feeling. Then he had to decide what his feelings meant and what to do about them. Finally, he had to learn how to express them. I worked with Rod on the following three experiments.

Experiment: Understanding and Using Feelings

1. Labeling Emotions and Letting Them Shift

Notice the peaks and valleys of your feelings during the day. Pay special attention to the sensations in your gut and label each feeling you experience. Restrict yourself initially to a simple emotional palette: mad, sad, glad, lonely and scared. Once you can consistently label these, add more, such as pride, humility, envy, safety, and love.

Whenever you experience a strong feeling, try breathing with it for a minute. Then scan slowly down your body from head to toe, feeling into each area from within (as compared to observing your body from your head). Notice what happens to your feelings and how they shift. Meditating with feelings in this way is different from reflecting on feelings. Reflecting is thinking about a feeling in order to evaluate it objectively. Meditating is experiencing feelings with your whole body.

Notice feelings of happiness. You will likely find the happiness of achieving goals tends to be fleeting. Afterward, you may move on to the next goal and repeat the process of chasing happiness. You can connect with an enduring happiness and contentment by uncovering who you are underneath your transient reactions, thoughts, and feelings. Sorting and sifting through your emotional reactions is a first step. This is like clearing away years of weeds and brush that have grown up and obscured the earth underneath. Most of us have accumulated a great deal of emotional baggage by not attending to our feelings in the moment, and so this healing process can take some time.

2. Moving from Meaning to Action

After labeling your stronger feelings and meditating with them, choose between the following options in deciding what to do:

- *Nothing.* Emotions often push us to take quick action. However, after sitting with a feeling for just a few minutes you may find it subsides. The feeling may have been an overreaction or personalization. Perhaps you realize why you were frustrated or realize acting impulsively would be destructive. As you practice staying with feelings you can get to know your vulnerabilities and develop greater patience with your reactions.

- *Further exploration.* You are not sure what to do, but need to reflect further or talk to someone to get more information. It is important to distinguish rumination from reflection. Reflection is an objective and self-accepting examination from multiple perspectives. Rumination is a repetitive self-recrimination that can lead to depression.

- *Expression.* Decide whether and how you need to express your feelings. The assertive communication experiment below offers suggestions.

- *Action.* What is the message of your feeling in terms of what you want and need? How can you plan to use the energy of your feeling constructively?

3. Assertive Communication

Once you become aware of what others are feeling you need to be careful not to take responsibility for their feelings. Trying to fix or take away other people's pain just creates additional pain. You need to keep your focus on taking responsibility for your own feelings and their impact. Asserting your feelings constructively is central to taking care of your needs and to protecting yourself by establishing your boundaries. Rod took assertiveness too far — he was so forceful in communicating his needs that he became aggressive. He would bowl people over, hurt their feelings and not respect their boundaries. The middle ground Rod needed to learn was mutual respect.

To know where he was on the assertive/aggressive continuum, Rod needed to ask for feedback. However, it was hard for most people to be direct with Rod given how intimidating he was. He needed to rely more on his inner barometer. Feeling helpless is generally a sign you need to be more assertive. Anger can indicate you need to protect yourself, but it can also easily lead to aggressiveness. When you feel angry the best thing is to hold the feeling in your awareness until it cools and you get clarity.

Do you have the patience to wait till your mud settles and your water becomes clear? Can you remain unmoving till the right action arises by itself?

— *Lao-Tzu*

Assertiveness skills are an extension of Focused Speaking. There are three keys to assertive communication:

1. speaking from your own feelings (using "I" statements can help)

2. being specific in describing the other person's behavior

3. refraining from judging the other person or assuming negative intent (often the hardest part)

It can be helpful to start with this script: "When you ... [describe the other person's behavior without judgment], I feel ... [name your feeling], because ... [explain the consequence of their behavior and its impact on you]." Before practicing assertive communication, plan what you want to say by writing out the three parts of the script.

◆ ◆ ◆

Rod learned to tune in to his feelings and take the risk of sharing them with his wife. She was thrilled with the new level of dialogue this opened up. Rod's success at home gave him the confidence to start noticing feelings at work. He started by tuning in to his feelings during meetings and then reflecting on the information they provided. His next step was to try to read what others were feeling.

Experiment: Empathy and Emotional Attunement

Adopt the perspective of an anthropologist and study the culture of your organization as if it were an unknown tribe whose language you do not speak. Try to intuit what colleagues are feeling and intending by paying attention to their nonverbal signals. Focus on facial expressions, glances, eye contact, tone of voice, mannerisms, gestures, and posture. With people closer to you, take this a step further by asking them if you are right with your hunches. Though every person's signals are to some extent unique, the facial and vocal expressions of most feelings are consistent across cultures.[7]

Notice the impact of your colleagues' feelings on your own. Tune in to the subtle feelings in your body, particularly in your chest and gut. How do you feel the impact of a colleague's frustration, expressed in a backhanded compliment or sarcastic comment? Can you feel a twinge in your stomach or do you have some other visceral reaction? Becoming more attuned in this way provides you with information that allows you to anticipate others' needs and behavior.

◆ ◆ ◆

Rod learned to read his colleagues' feelings and started to use that information. Rather than banging his head against a wall, he could gauge when to back off in the face of resistance. Unfortunately, Rod was also intent on using his insights about his colleagues' feelings to manipulate them and get his way more effectively. His greater emotional attunement was still in the service of his own single-minded agenda. I could not get him to soften his attachment to his own point of view or acknowledge that someone else's needs and goals might be as important as his own.

After Rod and I consulted with his boss, we decided that coaching had taken him as far as it could. His new software initiative was moving forward, if not with his peers' enthusiastic support, at least without their active interference. I am never satisfied when I know there is more someone can learn, but his colleagues were happy with the outcome and told me Rod was like a different person. While he would still fall back into bullying at times, his attempts to maneuver people emotionally were pretty transparent. As long as Rod was able to listen, his colleagues could actually tolerate working with him. And that felt like a miracle.

> I pay a lot of attention to body language on a number of different dimensions. In meetings I watch how people channel their tension into the movements of their hands. Are they relaxed and comfortable in themselves or tense and worried? I also notice if they show interest by leaning into the table, or disinterest by leaning back. Are they making an effort to be present and listen, or are they pretending to be engaged when they have really checked out?
>
> — *Director of Risk Management,*
> *Global Manufacturing Company*

Another client of mine, Tom, was able to take EI further. He was able to go beyond reading his own and others' emotions to using them to help build relationships and reach organizational goals. Tom was a successful Wall Street trader who had recently been promoted. He was likeable but subdued, having succeeded with a rational and logical approach to work and relationships. He told me that he was not thrilled about his promotion because he had been successful and content in his previous role. His new management responsibilities required him to make dozens of people decisions that were gray and fuzzy compared to the analytical process he was comfortable with as a trader. Being able to measure success in this new role was a significant concern for him.

I taught Tom mindfulness exercises and how to follow his breathing. Mindfulness training increased his awareness of the physical sensations that paralleled his feelings. He learned to recognize the butterflies in his stomach as anxiety and to read the heat on his face and hands as anger. He became interested in the research of biochemists that revealed there are neurotransmitters, hormonal and peptide receptors, throughout our body.[8] It appealed to his rational mind that there was a scientific basis for trusting the signals and intelligence provided by his gut feelings and intuitions.

> Sometimes I have an immediate visceral reaction to a person or situation that leads me to disagree with what is being said — without understanding why I am reacting that way. When this happens, I stop myself from reacting externally until I can figure out what I was feeling and why. What blocker is underneath that is preventing me from experiencing the feeling directly and thinking logically about the issue? It can help to call my husband and think through the situation out loud. Reflecting with someone else in this way enables me to get a deeper level of insight into what I am feeling and reacting to.   —*Jana Helmrich, HR Director, Coach*

I coached Tom for over a year, helping him turn his keen intellect to the challenge of reading his own and others' feelings. I knew we had turned a corner when he started getting curious about team culture and how to build morale. He designed creative approaches to ensure junior staff saw opportunities for upward mobility, and job-sharing options so he would not lose his most talented women when they had children. Tuning in to his team's feelings enabled him to develop a loyal following and his business started to take off. At the end of our work Tom told me he loved his new role and looked forward to the ongoing challenge of further developing as a leader. He knew how to keep learning, and he knew that his enhanced EI had transformed his impact.

We know that when we are under stress and emotionally raw we are more prone to be reactive, irritable, and insensitive. This is confirmed by research showing that the greater our stress, the less empathy we have.[9]

EMOTIONAL INTELLIGENCE, MINDFULNESS, AND STRESS

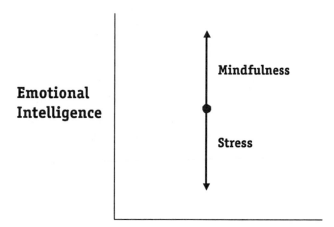

So as stress goes up, EI goes down. Conversely, mindfulness training reduces stress and anxiety, and thus is able to counteract the negative effect of stress on EI.[10]

As I mentioned earlier, mindfulness training increases empathy and the ability to read others' emotions.[11] In addition, mindfulness increases compassion and gratitude, along with activity in brain regions associated with positive emotion.[12] Mindfulness may thus enhance EI via a direct effect on brain function, as well by facilitating our ability to course-correct by giving us more information.[13]

We can enhance the information we receive by actively soliciting feedback from our network and personal board of directors. Having mentors and friends who will challenge our thinking with their own critical reflections expands our self-awareness by allowing us to see reality from other vantage points.

An important component of EI is using positive emotions to engage and motivate others. The impact of conveying a positive emotional tone in your body language and what you say cannot be underestimated. Research suggests effective leaders engage and coordinate their teams through these kinds of emotional signals and that specific neural pathways are involved.[14] "Mirror" and "oscillator" neurons in our brain may also be the basis for our ability to identify with and learn from leaders who model positive behavior. A positive focus and expression of emotions is contagious; it elevates everyone's mood and performance. Conversely, a leader's negative focus brings the whole team down. Managing your feelings and how you express them is thus critical.

During the financial crisis of 2008 the world's major banks lost billions of dollars. Markets swung wildly, and many people worked literally day and night to keep their firms from going under. The derivatives trading desk of one of my clients was run by a talented leader named Mary. After working straight through several nights in a row she was exhausted and raw. The next trading session was particularly grueling, with the market plunging hundreds of points. Mary knew she needed to rally herself and her team. If she could act as if she was confident, it could help her team not be paralyzed with fear. Mary marched calmly up and down the rows of the trading room, though she really felt sick from anxiety. She encouraged each trader, noticed good calls and stepped in to give decisive orders when she saw someone losing their cool or their focus. Not only did Mary survive the day, but her ability to stay collected and express emotions she did not feel helped her team earn back significant revenue. It also played a large role in keeping her firm in business.

Chapter 14

Relationship Building, Negotiating, and Networking

Allen was an experienced operations executive who was hired to revamp the back office of a multinational pharmaceuticals company. A few weeks after he was hired, Allen was told he had a new manager and would report one level further down in the organization. Matt was fifteen years his junior, with a lot less knowledge of operations, but he had established relationships in the company and was trusted by senior management. Getting layered shook Allen's confidence and caused him to withdraw. He put his head down and focused on solving technical problems in his function. He was good at this, and it made him feel valuable.

Allen had a lot of fires to fight. The operations group was not well organized, and the technology was old. He did not have a deep bench he could delegate to, and so regular errors kept him busy. Allen fell into a common habit when we are under pressure. He began to act as if transactions were more important than connections and tasks were more important than relationships. Obviously he needed to get things done, and all the tasks he was working on were important. He just needed to know when he was trading with colleagues and when he needed to focus on connecting to build longer-term relationships. He had begun building relationships with his team. But as a senior executive, he needed to make a MindShift toward building broad networks with large numbers of diverse constituents.

Relationship Building . . . . **Networking**
Building individual relationships with   Building a broad network of relationships
teammates, customers, and supervisors   with subordinates, peers, customers,
     superiors, vendors, board members,
     community and government representatives

$\longrightarrow$

Before he could do this, Allen needed to build a trusting relationship with Matt. As much as he tried to hide it, Allen showed his frustration and resentment toward Matt in passive-aggressive behavior. Allen took a long time to respond to emails, and he was always the last one among his peers to submit reports. Matt already felt threatened by Allen's experience and age, and this behavior just made things worse. For me to be able to help Allen see this pattern, I first needed to build a trusting relationship with him.

Relationships are built with mindful attention, understanding, and compassion.[1] This sounds unbusinesslike. Soft. But we know what it feels like when we can't get someone's attention and conversely how special we feel when we get a lot of attention. At home and at work, deep listening and attention lead to understanding. We feel powerfully connected to people when we feel understood and accepted by them. When we understand another person's motivations, values, and belief systems it leads to compassion. And compassion is the core of love.

I spent a number of hours listening deeply to Allen. I appreciated his experience in prior companies and got to know his skills and expertise in detail. I learned something of his childhood and family, and how he had to start over professionally when he had immigrated to the United States as an adult. Showing Allen I understood and accepted him without judgment enabled him to open up. Allen began to trust that I was his ally and that any feedback I gave him came from a desire to support him rather than an agenda to fix him. Allen's trust in me enabled us to talk directly about his passive-aggressive behavior without Allen becoming defensive. Giving Allen this insight showed him that I could add value. Acceptance, understanding, trust, and added value put my relationship with Allen on a firm foundation.

Allen took on the challenge of building a relationship with Matt. He realized he needed to reach out and show Matt that, rather than resenting him, he appreciated and accepted him as his boss. He also needed to be able to be vulnerable with Matt in order to undo any threat Matt felt. Allen created a development plan on the basis of the leadership assessment I conducted, and Allen and I met with Matt to review the plan. In this meeting Allen took a risk and became quite vulnerable. He shared a number of his personal struggles that were underneath the behaviors highlighted in the assessment. For example, Allen described how his constant self-criticism made it harder for him to be decisive.

Allen modeled the open relationship he wanted with Matt and gave Matt an opportunity to respond in kind. It was remarkable to see how quickly a distrustful, antagonistic relationship could change. Over the next couple of weeks Allen continued being vulnerable, asking for help and sharing himself, and the trust with Matt continued to grow. Being guarded and private could keep him from being hurt, but Allen understood that a "tough guy" persona would only end up putting Matt off. With the trust he had established with Matt, Allen was free to develop a broader network of relationships with senior executives above Matt, without Matt feeling uncomfortable.

Matt asked Allen if he would spearhead an initiative to consolidate international operations into one offshore location. In order to do this, Allen would need the support of multiple division heads. His challenge was to build a network of relationships with this diverse group of powerful individuals, all of whom would have to give up control of their own operations for the initiative to be successful. To accomplish this, Allen needed to learn the art of negotiation.

We start building relationships by listening, demonstrating understanding, building trust and supporting the other person's success. Then, over time, we strengthen those relationships by negotiating our respective needs and goals so that there are win/win outcomes. When both people go away satisfied, it makes each more likely to come back to the relationship for more. Creating win/win outcomes depends on our taking the other person's perspective. In other words, we need to shift our focus from our goals to the other person's, and to identify if there is a shared goal. Some people, like Rod (the former tank commander), struggle to shift away from their own agenda to a shared agenda. Rod could not build long-term relationships because he always took a win/lose approach. I win. You lose.

The **Goals–Enablers–Risks** model shown on the next page focuses on the human element of negotiation. This makes the model valuable for both relationship building and influencing. Other negotiations approaches focus on tactical positioning (e.g., Fisher and Ury's "Getting

GOALS – ENABLERS – RISKS

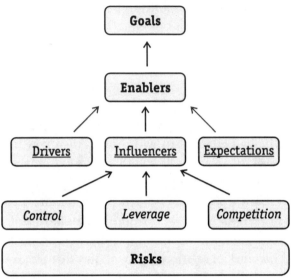

to Yes"), or on using mathematics and game theory to plot strategy (e.g., Dixit and Nalebuff's "Strategic Thinking" model).

The win/win negotiation process starts with establishing the relationship and clarifying shared **goals**. Allen could not simply reach out to the division heads and start negotiating. He needed to build a relationship with each one and establish that they both wanted to reach a common end point. He then needed to inquire into three **Enablers**: Drivers, Influencers, and Expectations. Drivers can be emotional or concrete. Many of the division heads had an emotional need to be treated with respect, for their expertise, role, title, etc. In other situations their driver was concrete (e.g., some resource, cost savings, or specific tasks they needed Allen's new organization to take on). Allen had to take all of their different drivers into consideration.

Influencers include *Control, Leverage, and Competition.* Allen had done a good job developing trust, but he had no *control* in the form of positional power or financial capital. Allen's only *leverage* came from borrowing his boss's power. He had a good relationship with Matt, and Matt's boss also wanted the initiative to succeed. With one division head

Allen also had leverage from a piece of embarrassing information which, if revealed, would hurt the division head politically. In terms of *competition*, the division heads had two other options besides Allen. They could keep the status quo as it gave them more control, or they could outsource their operations to a lower cost vendor.

There are many levels of <u>Expectations</u>, and this is an area where we often make costly assumptions. If Allen came to a meeting expecting to reach an agreement and the division head only wanted to understand his proposal better, Allen could go away disappointed. If a division head expected Allen's new organization would save him 15 percent, and Allen offered only 8 percent, the division head would be disappointed. However, if the division head expected a 5 percent savings, and Allen was able to offer 8 percent, he would be elated.

Risks make us hesitate and worry and can be both perceived and real. Many of the division heads risked losing "face" because they would be giving up staff to Allen. However, they did not raise this directly with Allen because they did not want to appear petty. Other division heads felt the biggest risk was Allen being able to deliver quality operational support with an unproven centralized model. Allen had to listen closely and actively draw out their concerns. In spite of his efforts, Allen still had division heads nodding their heads as if they were in full agreement, only to find them later stalling or blocking him behind the scenes.

Most of the time we are looking for a win/win outcome. If there is no shared goal, though, we may reasonably decide not to negotiate at all. In addition, if the relationship we want is not long term, and we can afford to never have to negotiate with this person again, then we may adopt a win/lose approach. In Allen's case he needed win/wins. He had no plans to retire early, and if the division heads were going to become his clients, he needed long-term relationships with all of them.

Allen developed a negotiation plan, which he adjusted continuously as he gained more information during each negotiation. Elements of his plan included techniques to remain calm, objective and logical, making sure he anticipated roadblocks, and coming up with ways to show personal support for all of his constituents. Allen also knew he needed to retain responsibility for execution. He could not afford to have his plans fall apart by assuming the division heads could get things done without his help. Shifting hundreds of staff from around the world to a centralized location was a huge change management effort that Allen's organization would have to lead.

Once Allen had mapped out all of the steps in the win/win process, he then had to think about tactical positioning. This included questions such as "What would be his starting offer in terms of proposed cost savings?" and "How far would he back down?" Typically, once the goals, enablers, and risks are mapped out, these tactical pieces fall into place more easily. Allen prepared some tactical plans in advance, but he found that the more he scripted these, the less likely he was to find creative alternatives during each negotiation. He wanted to remain as open as possible regarding the final plan for consolidation. He wanted to learn from the early rounds of negotiation and collaborate with the division heads on the final design.

It took Allen some time to get used to reflecting on shared goals and anticipating process factors and risks. With practice, though, it became more automatic. In addition, as he grew his organization and his people's capability, he was able to delegate more and free himself up. This got him out of the trap of rushing from meeting to meeting and trying to "wing it" in his negotiations. This would have made misunderstanding and conflict almost inevitable, and this is where Allen's time planning and reflecting paid tremendous dividends.

Conflicts are often a disagreement about approach rather than goals. In other words, we generally disagree about how to reach goals, not the goals themselves. Allen was able to sidestep a number of potential conflicts by demonstrating respect at the start of his negotiations and highlighting shared goals. This made the division heads relax and feel supported. The division heads genuinely believed Allen was trying to get to the same place, and so they were more willing to be flexible in following Allen's approach and going along with his plans for the consolidation. Relationship building and win/win negotiating are thus at the heart of influencing.

Conflicts can also occur when we personalize communication. One division head, Paul, assumed that Allen was going after his territory and interpreted his behavior as a personal attack. For his part, Allen got frustrated with Paul for not responding to his emails and then lost his cool when Paul complained about him to Matt. Matt came to Allen and beat him up for mishandling Paul. Allen then started to make erroneous paranoid assumptions about Paul trying to get him fired. Paul and Allen's teams also got into the act and started bickering with each other. Neither Paul nor Allen understood what the other was doing or why. They each took classic personalizing positions: Allen assailed Paul's character saying, "He's a jerk," and Paul maligned Allen's competence saying, "He's an idiot."

I helped Allen escape this downward spiral by asking him to step back and "professionalize" the situation.[2] Instead of focusing on character or competence, we focused on the specific goals, roles, and procedures in how he worked with Paul. He then reached out to Paul, apologized for the miscommunication between them, and objectively reviewed the pros and cons of consolidation rather than the other approaches to reaching Paul's goals. Paul took Allen's lead and retreated from his personalized stance. Allen proposed to Paul how they could clarify their roles and suggested more effective procedures for their teams to work together. Paul agreed to move forward with Allen's project.

Influencing within an organization often involves different groups lobbying for their particular set of interests. While politics has gotten a bad name, it is vital to an organization that each party with a vested interest speaks up about their needs so a complete picture can emerge. Politics become detrimental only when parties become unable to see each other's perspective and negotiate win/win solutions.

Early on in my career I needed to make decisions on my own. Now, it's not about my decisions, but about bringing all the key constituents across the organization together to make the best decisions. Facilitating a true dialogue and incorporating everyone's goals and needs into the solution brings the whole organization forward.

—*Elizabeth Dunlap, SVP, Chief People Officer,*
Panera Bread

Each division head wanted to make sure Allen's approach took their needs and drivers into consideration. Allen's consolidation was ultimately a success because he was able to balance all of these political interests while ensuring the consolidation still had enough efficiency to reduce costs. His project rolled out with all the division heads on board and now saves his organization between $100 million and $200 million each year.

Experiment: Win/Win Planning and Perspective-Taking

Think about an important project you are working on.

- Outline your goals, process factors, and risks.

- Outline the other person's goals, process factors, and risks, and make sure to identify if there is a shared goal.

- Try to view the problem from the other person's perspective. How does the meaning of the problem change if you look at the wider context the problem rests in? Consider the organizational, cultural, and familial context.

- Begin to create a negotiation plan.

◆ ◆ ◆

Experiment: Key Constituent Mapping

Numerous studies have demonstrated that effective leaders get results by building and maintaining a broad network.[3]

- Think about your top six to ten key constituents — people who you depend on and who depend on you.

- Rate the strength of each relationship, considering the level of trust, mutual understanding, and support experienced by each person.

- What action would improve each relationship?

- How could you clarify the goals, roles, and procedures in how you work together?

- How often should you make sure you are connecting with this person? Can you schedule meetings in advance or ask your assistant to do this so you don't have to remember to make each appointment?

Mapping your key constituents and having a plan for each person ensures your relationship building efforts are focused.

KEY STRATEGIC ALLIANCES AND RELATIONSHIPS

Name	Relationship	Actions/Critical Success Factors	Contact Frequency
Laura Lind	Senior Client	Manage function effectively	Quarterly
John Cash	Senior Client	Be CTO and assist in GLD success	Monthly
Greg Hines	Peer	Aggressively deliver Operating Plan	Monthly
Mike Toll	Peer	TBD	Bi-annually
Lily Foo	Peer	Reduce cost base and still deliver	Quarterly
Tim Mathews	Direct Report	Time/coaching on succession	Weekly
Orland Gibbs	Mentor	Involvement in my development	Quarterly
David Dodd	CFO Finance	Re-prioritize DGA/Implement	Quarterly
Ezra Stiles	CFO IB	Better MIS	Monthly
Hall Honde	Corp. Controller	Risk averse implementation	Weekly
Peg Goode	Domestic AD	Company centric/apolitical	Bi-annually
Allison Wind	CTO Office	Effective reusable strategy	Monthly

As you think about your key constituents, another dimension to consider is their "sphere of influence."

In trying to build relationships and influence, especially with hard-to-reach senior executives, it is helpful to think about who has their ear and whom they trust. Thus, branding yourself and developing your reputation becomes about adding value for the people around that person, i.e., people in their sphere of influence. This can become even more important than adding value directly to the person you are trying to reach.

— *Mark Matthews, Managing Director, Deutsche Bank*

Experiment: Collecting 360 Feedback

Schedule regular time with each of your key constituents to ask for feedback. Realize that giving feedback is hard, to say nothing of receiving feedback. You may need to ask multiple times before people trust that you really want to hear what they have to say.

- Make it easier on yourself and your constituents by asking them for advice about what you can do more effectively tomorrow, rather than what you did wrong yesterday.

- Ask them for feedback on your strengths and on when you are at your best. Too often we just focus feedback on deficits and weaknesses.

- Ask your constituents to give you immediate feedback whenever they see something that could help you. Contracting for ongoing feedback is one of the best ways to develop your relationships and build your interpersonal radar.

◆ ◆ ◆

Chapter 15

Leading and Developing Teams

You are standing in the center of a dark cave. You have a flashlight and turn it on. You are nervous and unsure of where you are, and your light shakes as you direct it around the huge empty space. You take a breath and notice the sensations in your body. Your hand starts to steady and you continue breathing. You can now direct the light where you want and see more clearly.

You notice your team members are with you. They are spread around the sides of a large lake in the center of the cave. Each person has a flashlight. Their lights flicker and are dimmer than yours. Flashes bounce around the ceiling as they begin to explore. Your light attracts their attention and they collect around you. As a group you now have enough light to see each other clearly. With your flashlight you are able to make out a path, and you start down it. Your team follows, the members using their own lights to make sure they don't trip and looking up to see yours every so often so they can stay on the path.

The first task in forming a team is to figure out where are you all going, in other words, to identify a shared goal. Leading the team is about managing the team's attention so everyone is focused on how to support and achieve that goal. To do this you must clearly articulate the team's direction and regularly communicate about the goal.

Larry looked directly at me. He had a problem and didn't know what to do. I had just finished reviewing his 360 report with feedback from his team, peers, clients, and senior colleagues. A clear theme was that he did not have a team. As the head of manufacturing for his company, he was managing each of his eight plants separately. Each plant manager competed with the others to see how many of the different cookies and cracker products they could make in their plant. The more products they

I often see teams struggling to come together because everyone is so distracted and their attention is going in a million different directions. Each team member is preoccupied with different individual issues and they are moving at light speed in different directions. So it becomes a challenge to have people connect on a common goal. We need to slow them down and focus them to get them to talk, listen, and agree. Even in front of our senior management, team members can't stop themselves from multitasking and checking their Blackberries! It is no wonder it is so hard to get teams to step back, be present, and prioritize key issues together.

—*Eileen Springer, VP, Strategic Talent Management and Enterprise Learning & Development, Pitney Bowes*

controlled, the more resources, new equipment, and staff they could get. I looked back at Larry. I didn't know what to do either. This was a group of experienced and tough individuals who had been operating this way for a long time. What would make them want to work together and cooperate?

Larry understood when I told him this would take significant time and commitment. We needed a lot more than a the typical one-day "feel-good" team-building event. The team would have to start meeting more regularly, in person, to build the relationships of trust required. This would be difficult because the plants were located around the country. We decided to meet every six weeks at a different plant. Each plant manager would have the opportunity to host a meeting. That manager would work with me and one other manager to design the activities and facilitate the meeting. This would include showing the group their facility and opening themselves up to suggestions from everyone about how to improve their operations.

This design ensured that the process of planning and preparing for each team meeting would itself begin to build teamwork. The plant mangers would have to begin learning to work together to create productive and engaging activities for the rest of the group. They would also have to start thinking about the team as a whole and how they could begin to be accountable to each other and depend on each other. In other words, they had to start sharing the leadership role with Larry rather than expecting all direction and communication to come from him.

The first team session went better than I could have expected. Larry made himself vulnerable, admitting that his leadership style was part of the problem and asking his people to push back if they saw him slipping back into directive management. He described how he had seen many bosses foster competition, but he now believed the team would be more productive if they pooled their resources and focused their energy on competitors in the marketplace rather than on each other. This was the start of a business case for teamwork. His team took his lead and began sharing their ideas and concerns about working more closely together.

In one activity we designed, each team member drew a picture of his or her plant's challenges on a flip chart. Then everyone went around the room and wrote suggestions and offers of concrete support on each picture. There was now a commitment to follow up and a process for them to develop relationships where they supported each other's growth and success after the meeting.

I was surprised as we rode to the airport that Larry was not more upbeat. He acknowledged that we had made a very good start, but he realized he had a number of major obstacles. First among these was that not all of his team members were strong enough. He was going to have to make some tough decisions, and he knew this would rock the growing sense of trust and safety within the team.

Larry objectively reviewed each person's strengths and weaknesses, being careful not to compare them to himself as the measure or to apply his personal value system. He did not want a team of clones who would not be able to see errors in the group's thinking. He needed a team with complementary skills and diversity in three broad categories:

- *Functional/technical skills:* the up-to-date knowledge, skills, and abilities needed to complete each job. With his experience, Larry was able to make this assessment pretty accurately, and two team members, Joe and Ryan, fell short.

- *Problem-solving style:* having people who think differently ensures that the team sees multiple perspectives and thinks creatively. There are hundreds of questionnaires designed to help individuals learn about each other's styles and improve communication. Some of these questionnaires have dubious utility, so it is important to have help picking one that is well constructed. We used a short questionnaire to assess each team member's thinking style. As might be expected with operations managers, everyone scored high on getting closure and getting things done. This group was at no risk for getting stuck in creative brainstorming.

- *Interpersonal preferences:* having diverse approaches to relationships helps teams complement and learn from each other. We used a simple personality assessment with straightforward scales measuring inter-personal and communication preferences. At senior levels I often see groups of extroverts who do not easily give people time to think on their own. Larry had a group of introverts. They had to be reminded to reach out and share their ideas and plans with each other.

I could work with the team to make sure the problem-solving styles and interpersonal preferences did not become a problem. But there was little I could do about the technical gaps. Moreover, Joe and Ryan were coasting. They were not motivated to learn new approaches at this point in their careers. At the next team meeting Larry orchestrated a face-saving retirement party for Joe and Ryan. It was elegant, but it was like watching a funeral. For a number of weeks there were reverberations of anxiety about who might be next. Larry anticipated this and reassured each remaining team member that they played a unique and important role on the team.

In addition to feeling safe relative to Larry, team members needed to feel safe with each other. In other words, they wanted to know if they would be accepted or judged. This was a high priority because Larry needed his people to stretch themselves and take risks. Larry learned to pay attention to signs of frustration and tension between team members. We were four months in, and he realized a clique of three of his more senior managers was beginning to form. They were starting to gossip about whether the initiative would survive, and whether some of the more junior members who were struggling would be let go.

Larry realized it was time to have a conversation about behavioral expectations and norms. In fact, perhaps we should have had this conversation with the team earlier. At the next team meeting Larry facilitated an open forum. Team members could raise any issue about how they wanted the team to work together going forward. I suggested a few questions to start us off:

- How will we handle conflict?

- What is the expectation regarding gossip? Was it okay to talk about people behind their backs?

- What is the standard for how quickly we needed to respond to requests from each other?

- How much will we share with individuals outside the team regarding our conversations with each other?

This provoked a lively discussion. Once these questions had been discussed and norms agreed, they were typed up and each team member signed the document. They decided to call it a "Declaration of Interdependence." It was a public commitment of mutual support. Of course this declaration was not enough on its own. Larry needed to model this behavior and hold people accountable. Larry privately confronted each of the members of the senior clique about their behavior and reinforced their commitment to the declaration. The gossiping stopped. His ability to handle difficult feelings and potential conflicts in this way increased the sense of trust in him as the leader.

As Larry developed his team he needed to shift his focus. He needed to step out of the action in order to facilitate and watch the dynamics of his whole team. Trying to view things from forty thousand feet gave him perspective and distance. In addition, Larry developed his emotional intelligence and interpersonal radar so he could observe and interpret team dynamics. Learning to use his gut intuition and feelings to read what was going on was essential, especially given that Larry was a literal and linear thinker. While he was very bright, there was no way he could *consciously* process all the subtle nonverbal communication that was going on at once in his team.

I understood intellectually what I needed to do to be an effective leader. But I wasn't able to do that until I understood what that meant to the people I lead in terms of the emotional impact. How did it feel to be led by me? Until I fully understood what my leadership felt like for them, I wasn't able to make the changes I needed to make.   — *Andrew J. Moss, HR Director,*
Global Consumer Products Company

An important MindShift Larry made was going from self-development to coaching and team development. Coaching individuals using focused attention is an art and science unto itself. However, the essence of developing members of a team is paying attention to each of them and their individual needs. A large part of your job is negotiating between each individual's needs and the needs of the organization. This means building relationships and negotiating a win/win outcome with each team member.

Self-Development . . . . **Coaching and Team Development**
Working toward your own personal   Selecting, delegating, motivating, and
and professional growth   developing others

--→

In addition to common needs (such as feeling safe and valuable), each of Larry's team members had unique needs. Therefore, Larry had to adjust his style and work with each team member differently. For example, some of Larry's managers had a strong need for autonomy. They wanted to be given a lot of room and to be able to check in with him only when necessary. Larry realized others team members did much better with more structure and clarity. Some of this had to do with the skill and developmental level of each individual (the senior managers wanted less support from Larry). However, a great deal was also a function of individual style and personality. Larry kept a bendable Gumby figurine on his desk to remind him of the importance of flexibility.

Before we started working together, Larry made most of the important operational decisions by himself. To develop his team, though, he realized he needed a more participative approach to decision-making. At one team session I reviewed the range of choices they had when an idea came up or a choice needed to be made:[1]

- No Response
  - A member suggests an idea and no one responds.
  - The group simply moves on without fully considering the idea.

- Formal Authority
  - The leader makes the call, or,
  - Someone the leader has authorized makes the call.

- Minority Rule
  - A vocal minority pushes a decision through.
  - The majority are too weak or passive to stop the minority.

- Majority Rule (Voting)
  - The numerical majority wins and celebrates.
  - The minority gets upset and tries to get even.

- Unanimity
  - Everyone has to fully agree before the group can take action.

- Consensus
  - Often confused with unanimity. The group can take action as long as everyone has been heard, and no one is so opposed to the decision that they cannot support its implementation. There is a "sense of direction or agreement."
  - This approach, practiced and developed most by Quakers, can take a great deal of time. However, there is often no substitute for the level of commitment this can generate.

Larry told the team that when time was tight, he would make a quick decision in the interest of efficiency. However, his goal was to develop the team's capacity for independent thinking and to align everyone's energy in the same direction. Thus, the best decisions would come from the group going as far as possible toward consensus.[2] Larry's team discussed a range of alternatives in the middle. For example, if there was not enough time for consensus, Larry could poll each team member on their views before making a decision (a cross between voting and the leader's call).

Experiment: Roles and Responsibilities Charting

A fundamental task in leading teams is ensuring clear roles and responsibilities. These often need to be reestablished over time as the team develops and integrates new members. A simple technique for accomplishing this is to create a roles and responsibilities chart.[3] The chart establishes how team members are involved in specific decisions and tasks. In addition, the process of charting identifies different perceptions and provides a process to reach agreements on accountabilities and roles.

Instructions and a template are shown below. Take a team through the exercise of agreeing on definitions and filling in the chart for their most important projects.

Instructions

- Use the R&R chart to identify decisions, tasks, or projects down the left-hand side. Across the top fill in the names of team members who are related to each decision, task, or project.

- Define mutually understood codes to describe the type of participation by each member. Develop your own codes using language that fits your culture. Some suggestions to get started:

  D = Decision Maker, must sign off before going ahead
  A = Accountable, the person to go to when an "accounting" or progress report is needed
  R = Responsible, provides input, support
  C = Consult, touch base before deciding
  I = Inform, notify after decision, input not needed

- Identify each team member's role by placing the appropriate letter in each box.

- Have each team member complete an R&R chart individually, indicating what they believe are the key tasks and their relationship to each using the codes you agree upon.

- Collect the data in advance of a team session, and then use the session to discuss discrepancies.

ROLES AND RESPONSIBILITIES CHART

PEOPLE

Projects, Programs, and Tasks

Traditional organizational boundaries of hierarchy, function, and geography are continuing to disappear as the world becomes more virtual and global. Shared decision-making approaches like consensus empower employees to grow and have input into organizational strategy. Leaders try to break down rigid boundaries because they make organizations less adaptable and responsive. Roles become more fluid as teams react to rapidly changing external environments. One team member often needs to play multiple roles on a given project.

Roles and responsibilities charting is an important first step to achieving clarity. However, this tool provides only a rough guide to navigating this new "boundaryless" organization. Leaders need to pay attention to internal, psychological boundaries that become more important in this context. To do this they need to focus on what is being overtly and covertly communicated by teammates about their needs for more or less authority, narrower or looser definitions of who does what, and clarity around who is in and who is out of the team.[4] When things go well, team members feel trusting, competent, and appreciated. When they don't go well team members feel mistrustful, ashamed, and inept. Your role as the team leader is to read these feelings, use them to diagnose problems, and help team members navigate these natural tensions.

◆ ◆ ◆

Experiment: High Performing Team Survey

With Larry's team spread around the country, it was difficult for him to accurately assess its ongoing functioning and stay on top of the adjustments needed to keep it on track. Surveying the team was a way to collect objective data and get the team to focus on specific dimensions. Reflecting on the feedback enabled them to self-correct.

Distribute the survey below to your team. Summarize the results for the team and plan a meeting to discuss the issues and generate solutions. Building on the work of Edgar Schein, I have included some of the most important dimensions of healthy team functioning.[5] You can change the format and dimensions of the survey to fit the specific challenges your team faces. The survey can also be given to individuals outside the team, for example, customers and key constituents elsewhere in the organization.

HIGH PERFORMING TEAM SURVEY

Rate the performance of the team on the following dimensions. Note both the current level of each competency you feel the group demonstrates with a "C" and the desired state you would like the group to achieve with a "D." In rating the desired state realize that we cannot expect to be a "10" for each competency and probably do not need to be in order to be an effective team. Additional space is provided after each item to expand on your responses. The team leader or facilitator will summarize responses to the open-ended items and share them with the group. No individual comments or quotes will be shared.

Name (Optional): _____   Date: _____

GOALS

Poor   1   2   3   4   5   6   7   8   9   10   Excellent

Confused; diverse; conflicting; indifferent; little interest.

Clear to all and shared; generate commitment and buy-in; individual and team goals aligned.

_____

_____

_____

_____

_____

COMMUNICATION

Poor   1   2   3   4   5   6   7   8   9   10   Excellent

Indirect; misunderstood; vague; scattered.

Direct; clear; good mutual understanding; to the point.

_____

_____

_____

_____

_____

PARTICIPATION

Poor   1   2   3   4   5   6   7   8   9   10   Excellent

Few dominate; some passive;   All contribute; all ideas/opinions
some not listened to; several   heard and considered.
talk at once or interrupt during meetings.

_____

_____

_____

_____

_____

FEELINGS

Poor   1   2   3   4   5   6   7   8   9   10   Excellent

Unexpected; ignored;   Freely expressed;
or criticized.   empathic responses.

_____

_____

_____

_____

_____

ESPRIT DE CORPS

Poor   1   2   3   4   5   6   7   8   9   10   Excellent

Friction and/or distance   Team is enthusiastic and enjoys
between team members;   working together; has a "can do"
poor morale.   attitude and high morale.

_____

_____

_____

_____

_____

DIAGNOSIS OF GROUP PROBLEMS

Poor   1   2   3   4   5   6   7   8   9   10   Excellent

Team jumps directly to remedial proposals; treats symptoms rather than root causes.

Problems carefully diagnosed before action is proposed; alternatives thoroughly considered; remedies address core issues.

_____

_____

_____

_____

_____

LEADERSHIP

Needs for leadership not met; team dominated by one or few leaders; power struggles for leadership.

As needs for leadership arise, various members meet them; anyone feels free to volunteer as team needs emerge; little competition for power.

_____

_____

_____

_____

_____

DECISIONS

Poor   1   2   3   4   5   6   7   8   9   10   Excellent

Needed decisions don't get made; decisions made by part of team; others uncommitted.

Consensus sought and tested; deviations appreciated and used to improve decisions; decisions are fully supported.

_____

_____

_____

_____

TRUST

Poor   1   2   3   4   5   6   7   8   9   10   Excellent

Members distrust one another; are polite; careful, guarded; listen superficially but inwardly reject what others say; are afraid to criticize or to be criticized.

Members trust one another; reveal to group what they would be reluctant to expose to outsiders; respect and use feedback; can freely express negative reactions without fearing reprisal.

CREATIVITY AND GROWTH

Poor   1   2   3   4   5   6   7   8   9   10   Excellent

Members and team in a rut; operate routinely; people stereotyped and rigid in their roles; little growth or personal support.

Team flexible, creative, and seeks new and better ways; individuals change and grow; individual growth supported.

INTERDEPENDENCE

Poor   1   2   3   4   5   6   7   8   9   10   Excellent

Team members operate on their own agendas and in the service of their own goals.

Members support each other and go out of their way to help each other, seeing their own success as necessarily linked to the team's success.

EXTERNAL RELATIONSHIPS

Poor   1   2   3   4   5   6   7   8   9   10   Excellent

Group is insular; blames other groups for problems; little interaction or collaboration with other groups.

Interaction is positive externally; group communicates and solves problems well with other groups.

_____

_____

_____

_____

◆ ◆ ◆

I worked with Larry's team for a year and a half. We administered the high performing team survey twice, once after four months and then again after a year. The first time there were a number of gaps between the current and desired state. However, before the group was able to have a productive conversation, some members began questioning the data. They wanted to see the exact distribution of scores on each item before they would accept what it meant. This threatened to bog them down, and I had to point out that, unlike settings on their production equipment, this was an area where directionally correct was more important than 99 percent precision.

"Participation" was solid as an overall average score, but write-in comments raised the issue that some members of Larry's team were quiet during meetings. We agreed the team needed to draw out these members and give them more time to have the floor. "Diagnosis of group problems" received low scores. As hands-on, action-oriented individuals, they did not spend much time diagnosing root causes. We identified one member of the team who was cautious and thoughtful and authorized him to slow the group down when he thought it necessary. Creativity had the largest gap between current and desired. They knew I had a passion for this topic, and so they asked me to run an innovation workshop at the next team meeting.

At the one-year mark we found significant improvements in the scores and smaller gaps between current and desired ratings. There were still issues that were raised, mostly in the written comments, and needed to be dealt with. However, the overall results were validating for the team, which was now more cohesive and confident in its ability to work together.

◆ ◆ ◆

There are innumerable activities to help teams work better together. Whether or not any one intervention is absolutely on target, the simple act of stepping back from our day-to-day transactional focus is healthy. Larry's team played a number of different team games and simulations and participated in some charity projects. At one meeting they went to a race track to watch how pit crews raced against the clock.

Of all these interventions, the single best way I have found for teams to develop is to do real work together. Larry's team developed the most from setting goals and developing their strategy, talking about how to support important projects, and brainstorming new ways to increase the efficiency of the plants. After focusing on each issue, we would take time to debrief and reflect on the process. Doing work in this way, with the explicit goal of improving how they worked together, resulted in sustainable improvements in the team's functioning. At my last meeting, I couldn't help smiling when a cynical gray-haired manager challenged the group during a debrief to address its real fears about an unexpected budget cut the company wanted the team to absorb. Larry caught my eye and smiled too. I knew our work was done.

Experiment: Planning a Team-Building Process

Identify a project your team needs to work on. Think about two or more team members who could help you plan and facilitate a session where the team can work on this project. Find somewhere away from your office so people get out of their normal operating modes. Have your facilitators organize other members of the team to tackle different pieces of the planning. One small team can handle the logistics of getting to and from the off-site. Another group can handle food and refreshments. Another group can find a way to bring fun into the event. Realize the process is the outcome. If your team can practice communicating and collaborating to plan the event, that itself will build teamwork. The lighter hand you take as a leader the better: facilitate the process rather than direct the outcome. Focus on observing the group dynamics and intervening to keep the group working well together.

Part III

Overcoming Five Destructive Habits

Overview

With practice, the skills you acquired in the last section will become a part of your leadership repertoire, and you will be able to flexibly apply each one. Unfortunately, under pressure you tend to fall back into old patterns and habits. Stress management and resilience techniques help protect you and keep new skills in place. It is also vital to understand the destructive habits themselves, including what locks them in and how to change them.

I start this section by explaining the nature of habits, which are pervasive in our lives. I then focus on five specific types of destructive habits and how to overcome them. The most common habit is a self-critical and perfectionist attitude toward yourself. This attitude undermines your ability to develop true self-confidence based on a core of self-acceptance. A related habit is negative and irrational thinking. We fall into a variety of negative thinking traps that do not allow us to see reality and possibilities clearly. You can undo these by cultivating a range of positive and self-reinforcing habits.

Uncertainty and change are constant features of our world. Our reaction to them is typically to freeze or run. Learning to get more comfortable with uncertainty helps you maintain your solidity and flexibility in the face of change. You cannot do without technology, and yet your dependency on it is a habit. Technology gets you moving faster and faster; multitasking becomes a habit and you lose your ability to focus. You overcome the destructive habits with positive habits such as setting limits, establishing boundaries, and sticking to priorities. Another success factor is learning to manage yourself rather than trying to manage time.

In this section I have included "failure stories" as well as "success stories." Our habits are often the reason we fail, and failures can offer more opportunities to learn.

Chapter 16

Habits

The paradox is that we have free will but are in many ways creatures of habit. If we focus on it, we can consciously choose how we think, feel, and act. Yet much of our behavior is initiated unconsciously, automatically, and repetitively. In other words, it is a habit.

Our brain consciously processes around eighty bits of information per second. Outside of our awareness, the rest of our brain is working on some eleven million bits of information per second. Much of this processing is devoted to things like visual pattern recognition, balance, and the maintenance of internal homeostasis, which you are probably quite happy to delegate to the reptilian centers of your brain. **In total, as much as 95 percent of your daily activities may be unconsciously determined.**[1]

Habits can be quite helpful in that they allow us not to have to think about every choice we face on a daily basis. What time to go to bed, when to get up each morning, brushing our teeth after meals — all these are healthy habits. Habits reduce the uncertainty of life and thus help us manage anxiety. However, when our lives become too full of habits, we become less conscious and able to make choices.

How we talk, react to criticism, interact with others, even the type of snack we instinctively reach for — all are habits.[2] Our automatic thoughts are habits. When you start to pay more attention to your conscious thinking patterns, you may find an even more worrisome fact. Our conscious thoughts can also be largely repetitive. Taking this to the logical extreme, Buddhists argue that our whole personality and sense of self is a set of habits and should therefore be taken much less seriously.[3] A personality based on habits is certainly a fiction to be distrusted.

As social animals we model what we do on our neighbors and become caught up in the rhythms around us.[4] New Yorkers do everything with a frenzy of activity, including shopping and playing. I feel like I have to run to keep up. As Dave Barry writes, it is a rule for New Yorkers to always walk at least thirty miles an hour and never make eye contact. New York's rhythm is driven by its commerce — the speed of millions of daily financial transactions on Wall Street.

It can be depressing to think that much of our behavior is unconscious and repetitive. The good news, though, is that we can strengthen our conscious willpower and start to slow the momentum of our habit flywheel.

Experiment: Paying Attention to Habit Cycles

The first step in changing habits is to pay attention to them. Pick a habit you would like to change and start to watch it. Notice three steps: (1) where and when you start the habit, (2) what you are feeling, and (3) what sustains the pattern. There are situations when we are more likely to engage in the habit (step 1). These often stimulate uncomfortable feelings like anxiety that make us want to engage in the habit (step 2). Engaging in the habit serves to reduce our anxiety (at least in the short term), thus sustaining and reinforcing it (step 3). Turning mindfulness toward this pattern can help interrupt it. Journal what you learn for a week, and see if paying closer attention starts to alter the cycle. Remember to be patient — self-criticism and judging can reinforce the negative feelings that fuel the habit.

◆ ◆ ◆

Experiment: Charting Habits

Pictures have great focusing power because of how visually oriented we are. Create a simple chart to track the frequency of a behavior you would like to change. You can graph a bothersome habit or track progress toward a goal. For example, you can use a chart to bring more attention to what you eat. Each day graph how many calories you take in and your weight. Add symbols to indicate negative as well as reinforcing events so you can get a clearer picture of the entire sequence. For example, notice if passing a doughnut shop on your way home triggers a desire to give up on your diet for a couple of days. Watching the graphic picture emerge is motivating and will increase your focus, which in turn will make you more aware while you are eating.

◆ ◆ ◆

As a 408-pound executive, Jesse was convinced his weight would limit his career. His doctors were convinced it would limit his life. Jesse tried paying attention to how he felt after he ate different amounts and kinds of foods, and I asked him to pay attention to each movement as he brought food to his mouth. We talked about recording his daily caloric intake, and we brainstormed ways he could get more exercise. It didn't work. There always seemed to be reasons why he couldn't do the things we talked about. He was too heavy to weigh himself on any scale, and he couldn't use the gym because he didn't want people staring at him. There appeared to be deeper issues getting in his way and he did not want to explore them. Sometimes increasing awareness is not enough to change engrained habits.

I met with Jesse a number of years later and was shocked to see how thin he was. He had lost 138 pounds. He explained that he had realized he had a fatalistic attitude about his health. "I stopped caring what people thought," he said. "If I was so overweight then I must be sick in all sorts of ways." What was the point of dieting if he was going to die soon anyway? Jesse scheduled a complete medical workup and it showed he was in fact not "all bad." Then his wife started the ball rolling, losing some weight herself, and seeing her success helped him believe it was possible. Having a partner who would eat the same healthier foods was a big plus. Jesse and his wife now weigh each other each morning and cheer each other on. He drinks 64 ounces of water a day and focuses on portion control. "We changed negative feedback loops into positive feedback loops," he told me. He sees positive impacts of being lighter all around him. He has even noticed that he gets better gas mileage.

We can try to change habits with effort, in other words by simply trying to stop cold turkey. However, it is extremely difficult to keep this up because our habits are self-reinforcing. They help us relieve anxiety, distract us from other uncomfortable feelings, and produce momentary pleasure. Because of their hold on us, when we force ourselves to stop, the habit often reasserts itself and gets stronger.

An easier way to change a habit is to introduce a new behavior to replace it. For example, breathing when the phone rings replaces the habitual startle response with a relaxation response. If you are trying to change your golf or tennis swing, you can start by paying close attention to the new movement and intentionally repeat it until it becomes natural and less effortful.[5] You will feel uncomfortable with the new motion at first, but in time it feels quite normal, and going back to the old way feels strange. Your attitude is as important as practice. Try to relax and be aware of pressing or judging. Being patient and letting go of expectations will facilitate your progress. Anticipate some backsliding so you do not get frustrated with yourself. Simply observe yourself and repeat the correct behavior without judgment.

I have focused on the inside out approach: expanding awareness of our range of choices in each moment. Here we are adding outside in approaches: trying on new behaviors and, with repetition, becoming more internally comfortable with them. We take the outside in approach when we read books about ideal leadership behaviors and try to emulate them. We use the same method when we model the behavior of a boss or mentor we admire. This approach has a great deal of value. However, you will have more sustainable success when you complement this with inside out approaches.

Is life a game for which there must be rules?
Are they from the outside in or inside out?
—*Ann Hunter Keefe*

Bernie was heading human resources for a multinational consumer product company when his company merged with a large competitor. Bernie was thrown into a horse race with the other HR head, Scott, for leadership of the combined function. Scott was aggressive and came out of the gate with a number of ideas to cut costs and staff. He criticized

Bernie publicly for being out of touch and leading a fat organization. Bernie was many years Scott's senior, but he was intimidated. I coached Bernie to act "as if" he were confident. He needed to avoid taking the bait, personalizing the attacks, or responding with mudslinging. He acted poised and presidential and soon started to feel more confident. He calmly responded to Scott's suggestions with his own rational arguments and plans. Bernie was ultimately chosen to lead the function, and the CEO mentioned his maturity during the merger as a central reason. Bernie had acted as if he was already in the role and worthy of it, and exhibiting this attitude gave the CEO confidence to put him in it.

Addictions are a particularly difficult and destructive habit. Addictions are mood-altering relationships with an activity, person, or substance that lead to life-damaging consequences.[6] Most of us have some type of addiction. We overuse a whole range of things including food, nicotine, caffeine, alcohol, drugs, sex, and work. The function of addictions is most often to avoid facing painful feelings such as anger, loneliness, self-loathing, and shame. Even relatively innocuous nervous or obsessive habits can have an addictive quality when we use them as ways of avoiding dealing with an internal dis-ease.

Experiment: Taming Addiction

Habituation is the habit of tuning out to external stimuli as well as tuning out to yourself. The first step in undoing addiction is to use positive sensitization to get back in touch with what you are feeling. You can do this by mindfully attending to what you are experiencing at a visceral level at the same time as you actively *refrain* from the addictive behavior.

• Pick a behavior you are addicted to and begin refraining from it. You will likely start feeling an immediate craving or itch.[7] You may feel a tension or tightening, and then an almost irresistible urge, discomfort, and restlessness.

• There are three typical responses: (1) to avoid and distract yourself (numb out); (2) to lash out (at yourself or others); or (3) to crave something (habit or substance) that will make the feeling go away.

• The alternative is to go into and stay with the discomfort and uneasiness. Like when you have been bitten by a mosquito, you need to stop scratching for the itch to subside.

The experience of refraining can feel like taking a great personal risk because of the anxiety it produces. **Overcoming addictions and habits is thus fundamentally about learning to tolerate discomfort and uncertainty.** Developing mindfulness helps you hold feelings in awareness so you do not depend on the addictive behavior to calm yourself.

◆ ◆ ◆

Cultivating positive habits, self-reinforcing rituals, and routines is as important as managing negative habits. For example, eating smaller portions of healthy food can have a strong effect on your mood and energy, which can quickly become a self-reinforcing habit. Try arranging your schedule so you exercise the same times each week, and you don't have to push yourself or remember to exercise. Feeling the effect on your energy (to say nothing of the addictive rush of your body's endorphins) makes you want to keep the exercise habit going. When I make sure to keep a full glass of water in front of me on my desk, I am more likely to drink and keep myself hydrated and alert. When the glass is not there, I forget about it and don't drink.

Most of us feel a natural lull in the afternoon and can have trouble continuing to work productively. I avoid caffeine because I don't want to become dependent on it and because it makes me jittery and less able to sleep. My afternoon restlessness often ends up turning into a craving for snacks. I used to keep candy in my desk, but it provided only a short boost and a few minutes later I crashed and needed more candy. I tried cherry tomatoes, carrots, and fruit. At first they were not that satisfying as a substitute, but after a while I started to appreciate their flavor and positive impact on my mood. Tomatoes and fruit are not very portable, so I keep a mixture of almonds and dried cherries on hand, and if I get a snack craving they are just the trick.

Chapter 17

Perfectionism, Self-Criticism, and Self-Confidence

Perfectionism is the myth that something better, an ideal, exists outside ourselves. If we drive hard enough, we can reach it, and then we will feel good about ourselves. Believing the myth, we spend our lives desperate to get better, smarter, more successful, wealthier, and more attractive. We look for the perfect career, perfect family, and perfect life. Unfortunately, we are never satisfied because our imagination can always picture something better just out of reach. The contentment we feel when we get what we want on this treadmill tends to be fleeting. There is never enough and never good enough.

Comparing ourselves to an impossible standard we always come up short. So we criticize ourselves for not being smart enough, pretty enough, or motivated enough. Occasionally we try to prop up our self-esteem with false bravado, but underneath is a big vacuum. Ultimately we need to realize that we cannot build a solid sense of identity and security from recognition and accomplishments. The problem is that there are so many factors in life we do not control, and so an identity founded on external success is not sustainable.

> Everything I care about is of the nature to change.
> I cannot prevent loss and separation from them.
> — *Thich Nhat Hanh*

We identify with our professional roles and status. As a result, we feel empty when we lose a job and have to reimagine ourselves. Our individualistic orientation makes us long for love, connection, and acceptance.

In spite of this we continue to chase status. As Warren Bennis says, "We dream of community and democracy but practice individualism and capitalism." This is because democracy fuels individualism, and individualism breeds fear and self-doubt. A vulnerable, isolated ego is not just an inescapable feature of the human condition. More collectivist cultures in the East seem to be spared much of the self-hatred we experience.[1]

Because perfectionists expect themselves to always succeed, they are more likely to get depressed after failure. In the stress research I referenced earlier, individuals with self-critical and perfectionist attitudes experienced greater physiological reactivity and more negative emotions after failing.[2] In addition, individuals with perfectionist attitudes are more likely to have self-critical automatic thoughts after failure, which lead to feelings of depression and worthlessness over time.[3] Perfectionist attitudes exacerbate our reaction to stress because they make us more likely to take failure as a sign of personal defect. When we see signs of this defect, we start analyzing ourselves and ruminating on how we can fix it. This is when reflection can become destructive.

We are especially prone to perfectionism and self-criticism because we cultivate consumerism to sustain our economy. If we were satisfied with the products we had, we would not buy enough new products for companies to grow. If companies don't grow fast enough we get disappointed, and when we don't get our 10 percent annual return, we sell our stock. We are also encouraged to engage in comparison shopping. This is the habit of looking at other people and external benchmarks to decide what we should think, feel, and buy. Every time we compare how well we are doing with how well others are doing we come out the loser. Advertising plays on our sense of deficit, claiming, "Your life cannot be complete until you have this product."

We were trained as children to position the ideal we are looking for outside ourselves, and we were taught to focus on outcomes (goals) rather than process (how we get to goals). We learned that winning the race and getting recognition for being the best were what counted most. Unfortunately this makes us vulnerable to feeling bad about ourselves because in most contests there are only a few winners. When we focus on process, we are more likely to experience and enjoy the journey and to feel good about ourselves and our learning along the way. Focusing on outcomes teaches us to live in future expectation and dooms us to disappointment. Focusing on process rather than outcomes enables us to build lasting self-confidence.

The curious paradox is that when I can accept myself just as I am, then I can change.   — *Carl Rogers*

Schools teach us that our job is to get good grades, not to enjoy the process of learning. Good grades will enable us to get into good colleges, which will enable us to get good jobs. Then we enter the corporate world, which is even more explicitly focused on outcomes. We can get a good bonus if we hit our numbers and get a good performance rating. There is no emphasis on the means to the end, only on achieving the end. As a result, we take whatever shortcuts we think are necessary. A few courses in ethics will not change this systemic problem.

Focusing too much on outcomes makes us impatient and gives us a low tolerance for frustration. In addition, it makes us nervous about the possibility of failure. When we tense up ("psych ourselves out") we perform poorly. In sports, when we focus too much on winning, we take our eye off the ball and miss the shot. John Wooden, arguably one of the greatest basketball coaches in history, exhorted his players to never look at the score. Instead, he wanted his players to focus on executing the behaviors and skills that would lead to the winning score. Focusing on execution in this way is focusing on process.

A number of studies have shown that the pressure we put on ourselves to avoid failure is associated with reduced learning motivation.[4] This makes sense because overfocusing on outcomes makes us worried about evaluation and thus less likely to engage in trial-and-error learning.[5] Learning is scary because it involves taking risks and potentially letting go of closely held beliefs, attitudes, and behaviors. However, we can retrain ourselves to value the concept of healthy failure. Seeing failure as feedback and an opportunity to learn makes us more resilient and productive following setbacks.[6]

It is important to recognize that process rather than outcomes is not an either/or choice.[7] As we will explore more in the chapter on goal-setting, establishing a target can be very useful and motivating. In addition, focusing on outcomes and goals is certainly better than focusing on problems. The problem lies in getting too attached to goals and losing our ability to stay with process along the way.

Experiment: Replacing Worrying with Planning

Worry is future-focused, unproductive rumination. Planning is present-focused problem-solving and goal-setting. If you find yourself distracted by worries, commit to planning at a specific later time. For example, rather than worrying off and on for hours about how you will do your taxes, decide that at 8:00 p.m. Tuesday you will spend thirty minutes planning and collecting records. Scheduling time to focus on problems is a very effective way of bringing yourself back to the present and engaging in productive activity process.

◆ ◆ ◆

When activities are intrinsically rewarding we learn a great deal and perform to the limits of our ability. However, when someone offers to pay us for the same activities, our enjoyment and performance can go way down. We make play into work by evaluating it and focusing on performance outcomes. I experienced this when I started my career as a violinist. At first playing gigs was great fun. I was fifteen and excited to be playing with much more experienced professionals. The more I thought about the violin as a career, though, the less fun it became. The musicians around me were also stuck in a terrible bind. They had not developed other skills and thus had to play to make a meager living. Their passion for playing music was still evident, but the necessity of playing to make money took much of the joy out of it for many of them.

Of course, money is also a powerful motivator, and generally when we are paid for something it increases how hard we work for it. However, money can quickly become the central reason for doing work, and we can lose our intrinsic enjoyment. For many professionals, money becomes a yardstick to measure self-worth. We cannot help feeling good about ourselves when we get a big bonus, and bad about ourselves when we don't.

The antidote is to refocus on more stable, internal measures — appreciating ourselves for who we are as people, our values, inner qualities, relationships, contributions to society, and positive impact on others.

Learn to recognize the counterfeit coins
That may buy you just a moment of pleasure,
But then drag you for days
Like a broken man
Behind a farting camel.   — *Hafiz*

The hierarchical nature of many organizations creates a hyperfocus on promotion. Unfortunately, the leadership skills required at the next level are often not the focus of the promotion process. Rather, things like your recent wins and the size of your organization and budget (your "platform" or "empire") get greater weight.

Jim was a marketing VP in a publishing company. At the end of the year he was told he would not be promoted to SVP because he lacked the leadership skills expected. He did not understand what this meant. After all, he had hit all his numbers. His boss, Lee, had difficulty explaining the behavioral standard and did not know how to help him change his command and control style. Lee offered Jim an executive coach to help him. Jim met a number of coaches and decided to work with Peter, an experienced and skilled colleague of mine.

Jim was initially wary of Peter but saw coaching as a means to get promoted, so he went along. After three months his direct reports saw some changes. He was able to become more aware of behaviors that were counterproductive and was clearly making an effort to listen rather than dictate. Change takes time to solidify, so it was decided to continue the coaching for a few more months.

After six months Lee met with Jim and Peter to review what Jim had learned. The three of them agreed to discontinue the coaching. Lee realized that Jim was just going through the motions. He was very motivated but by the wrong thing. He was not curious about himself or genuinely interested in learning. He just wanted to get promoted. Thus, he could not do more than robotically enact behaviors he thought were expected and was not truly integrating the learning.

Experiment: Getting into "Flow"

Think of an experience when you were deeply engaged in an activity, so much so that you lost track of time. Being in "flow" or "in the zone" is associated with peak performance in the arts or athletics, but it can occur whenever you are completely absorbed in what you are doing. This intense state occurs when you lose your self-consciousness and focus completely on your process in the present.[8] Recall the setting and events that led up to your experiencing flow. Think about any aspects of the setting that you could re-create.

- Choose an activity and try getting into flow for at least thirty minutes. You can use this to make something that feels like "work" back into "play." It can help if there is a creative element to what you pick, but even something as mundane as washing clothes can become a very different experience when done with complete absorption.

- Continually bring yourself back to the present and focus intently on the experience of what you are doing. Be aware of taking yourself out of the moment by judging yourself, anticipating the project being finished, or worrying about unrelated tasks. Also don't *try* to enjoy what you are doing — the emotional effort and evaluation of, "Am I enjoying this or not?" or "Am I in flow yet?" can quickly take you out of the process.

♦ ♦ ♦

You cannot control whether you will achieve all the outcomes you want in life. However, you can control whether you stay focused on process. You can control your effort to do your best in each moment and how much of the rest you let go.

Learning to trust the guidance of your feelings and gut instincts can help a great deal in learning to trust process. Staying present with your feelings is an important way of staying with process, and it is the basis of many psychotherapies. You begin to develop self-confidence when you learn to trust that your feelings will help you navigate through difficult challenges. Trusting your gut is a central part of trusting yourself.

Is it logical that you would be walking around entirely orphaned now? The truth is you turned away yourself and decided to go into the dark alone. Now you are tangled up in others, and have forgotten what you once knew.... —*Kabir*

Whenever you are in touch with your experience and feelings you are in process. When you lose contact with this part of yourself you can get into your head or caught up in other people or problems around you. You can then waste a great deal of time and effort trying to influence outcomes that are outside of your control. This doesn't mean you cannot help others. It just means you are much less helpful when you are not in touch with all of yourself.

Along with doing your best to focus on process, you can control how you treat yourself along the way. True self-confidence is built from a combination of trust in process along with self-acceptance.[9] Again, self-acceptance does not mean passivity, complacency, or self-indulgence. It means honestly facing and appreciating what is and developing a basic warmth toward yourself.

Creating self-acceptance is essentially about turning friendliness and compassion toward yourself.[10] Mindfulness practices emphasize open, accepting attention, and are a proven way to cultivate greater self-acceptance.[11] Self-acceptance is also supported by undoing negative and irrational self-talk. An enduring sense of self-confidence and well-being ultimately depends on building a positive, supportive relationship with yourself.

Chapter 18

Negative and Irrational Thinking

I recently met a very experienced consultant who was transitioning from compensation and organizational design work into coaching. Margaret had all it takes and more. However she doubted her skills. At the end of the meeting we exchanged business cards, and as Margaret brought hers out she said, "You are going to laugh at me again." I felt a twinge of pain in my gut as I heard her put herself down. I had, in fact, done nothing but validate her competence and strengths the whole time we were together, but she was embarrassed about calling herself a coach.

Our core irrational belief is that there is something wrong with us. This sense of basic defect contributes to perfectionism and self-criticism, which further undermine our self-confidence. Our sense of being flawed also leads to a pervasive and irrational negativity in our attitudes and thinking. Like Margaret, we expect criticism and look for negativity everywhere around us.

We crave recognition, appreciation, and approval. However, our attention is attracted to negativity. Our negative culture makes it even harder. News of disasters and death increases TV and newspaper interest, economic fears draw us close to CNBC, and negative advertising sinks political candidates. Being surrounded by these messages further reinforces our negative habit.

Other cultures can remind us that worry and a deprivation mind-set are not necessities. For example, the Mokens are peaceful nomads with their own unique language and sense of time. They live almost entirely on boats off the coast of Burma and Thailand in relative isolation from modern civilization. In their language there are no words for "when" or "worry." They survive by fishing and know any extra baggage will tie them down. They want very little and don't even have a word for "want" in their language.[1]

Cognitive psychology was developed to deal with irrational thinking. The premise is that we feel better when we replace negative and distorted thinking with more positive and rational alternatives. Many of our negative distortions come from identifying with and becoming fixed on thoughts rather than maintaining openness. This is where cognitive psychology comes close to beginner's mind.

When I heard Margaret put herself down, I asked her if she heard what she said. We talked about the impact this might be having on her confidence, and she agreed. She recognized it could help a great deal to try to notice these thoughts before she expressed them. When she notices these thoughts, she now plans to remind herself of all the experience and credibility she actually brings as a coach.

Rather than challenging or reframing negative thoughts, mindfulness approaches suggest we develop detachment and distance from them. The idea is to observe our thinking in order to see our distortions more clearly. Once we develop detachment, our thinking loses its ability to hook us. As Simon, the retiring mail services executive, said, "Mindfulness helps you not get on that runaway thought train brain."

Experiment:
Keeping a Rational Thinking Journal

Turn your attention to your thinking and listen in for a few days. Just below the level of awareness you will begin to hear a relatively nonstop conversation with yourself. Psychologists call this often irrational and negative chatter "automatic thoughts."

* Start to track this stream of thinking and journal the themes. If you notice a particular recurring thought, write it down and examine it more closely. See if you can gently challenge it and replace it with a more rational and positive alternative. Notice the emotional impact of reframing your thinking in this way.

- Become aware of using "musts" and "shoulds." How rational is it that you really have to do these things? Refocus on what you really care about, and see if you can replace each "must" or "should" with a "want" or "can." Notice if shifting from a "must" to a "want" makes you feel less burdened and more motivated.

- Assumptions are the largest category of thought distortion. Filling in gaps is adaptive because reality is gray, and we need to make sense of it to make decisions. However, we often fill in missing pieces with irrational expectations and fears. Reflect on a difficult situation you are facing and examine your thinking about it. What assumptions are you making about it and the people involved? See if you can bring a beginner's mind perspective. Start with the premise that you know nothing and try to build a more accurate picture of the situation. Flag any assumptions you are making along the way.

- Personalization is the most common type of assumption. Without judgment, think about how much you may be still carrying the natural egocentrism you were born with. It is natural to look at events and ask what they mean for you. However, how often do you assume that the way people are treating you is personal? Most of the people who insult or mistreat you are not at all focused on how they impact you. They are simply too preoccupied with their own needs to care about slighting you.

Be careful about the attitude you take to yourself and your thoughts. You may become self-critical when you notice persistent negativity, which will only fuel more internal conflict and stress. **Cultivating an accepting attitude toward yourself is the most powerful way to undo cycles of negative and irrational thinking.**

Anxiety takes a lot of attention. Rational thinking and mindfulness free up your thinking and enable you to look objectively at your resources and the real likelihood of imagined catastrophes. Focusing more effectively reduces feelings of fear, frustration, and sadness because it helps you shift your attention away from negativity.[2]

◆ ◆ ◆

Experiment: Deactivating Core Fears — the NO FEAR Approach

Pick a common theme in your worries and work through the following steps:

N Name the fear. For example, "I am afraid of losing my job"

O Objectively look beneath this worry by asking "What is the worst thing that would happen if that worry were to come true?" In the example of losing your job, perhaps the worst thing that would happen would be that you would have to explore new jobs and types of work. Now ask what is the worst consequence of that? Perhaps your underlying fear is that you will now have to ask people for help as you network. Keep going until you feel you have gotten to the bottom of the chain of consequences.

F Find a way to make peace with your worst fear and come to terms with it. Is it really as bad once you look at it directly? In this example, perhaps losing your job would allow you to broaden your identity and use more of your skills.

E Elaborate the learning. Reflect on the different ways the fear has been blocking you. Let your imagination help you create a new picture of your life that does not include this fear.

A Anticipate situations where the fear may get activated again. Plan ways you can check yourself and stop the fear from undermining you.

R Replace negative, irrational thoughts and beliefs with more positive ones. Each time you deactivate a fear by looking into its core, it strengthens your ability to stay focused and positive.

◆ ◆ ◆

For many years psychology devoted itself to alleviating mental illness, pain, and suffering. This has recently been balanced by the positive psychology movement, which is focused on how we can become happier and more fulfilled. For example, positive psychologists study how, especially when there is no direct benefit to us, we feel better when we make others feel better. The idea that "giving is receiving" is a core principle of most religions and has now been proven by a significant body of research.[3]

The intention behind giving is also important. We give and get much more when we give unconditionally and with the intention of creating happiness, as compared to giving grudgingly.[4]

A good friend of mine recently told me how his wife had started volunteering at a local hospice. She regularly went to visit a man who was dying of lung cancer caused by breathing in toxic fumes after 9/11. Rather than being saddened by the tragic experience, my friend described how much his wife was getting from it. She was becoming increasingly forgiving, patient, and open-hearted. This was not why she kept going. It just felt good to her, and the dying man and my friend got to enjoy her kindness.

Experiment: Cultivating Positivity, Perspective, and Gratitude

Positive psychology suggests that we reflect in specific ways in order to a change our attitude:

- At the end of each day, try thinking of all the good things that are going on in your life. Single out three things you are especially grateful for.

- Build up your service orientation by regularly asking, "How can I help?" or "How can I serve?"

- If you find yourself stuck worrying about a problem, examine your expectations. Are you becoming impatient to get to an outcome when there is a process you could follow and trust?

- If you are stuck on a painful feeling, try to get perspective by asking yourself, "Will I care about this in a month, or in a year?"

◆ ◆ ◆

As we discussed with emotional intelligence, a leader's positive mood is quickly picked up by her team, and vital for their performance. Positive emotions help us maintain resilience, buffer us from the impact of stress, and aid in recovery from daily stressors.[5] Conversely, negative moods are also contagious and resonate throughout groups long after their expression. Beware of pity parties that are all about "venting"; they often only strengthen negative feelings.

Recently positive approaches to consulting have started to gain more acceptance. Appreciative inquiry is based on the idea that organizations can change more easily when they focus on strengths and opportunities rather than problems and obstacles.[6] Positive perspectives also help when working with individuals. People who come to a coach or therapist with a positive attitude get more from the process.[7] Coaches who build on a client's strengths and existing resources are more effective because they build momentum, hope, and confidence in the process.

Annie was a talented financial services executive. She was creative and insightful, having little use for traditional approaches or established rules. She could also be charming and engaging, which made the dramatic changes she initiated whenever she went easier for colleagues to take. She rose up the ranks rapidly and was actively recruited to a new firm every few years.

Annie had a family with two children, but her work was the core of her identity. She thrived on the attention and accolades she received. Underneath she felt like a fraud. The imposter syndrome caught up with her when her firm decided that the new project she was leading was not core to their business.

Annie was devastated by being let go. Her first reaction was shock and then depression. After a few weeks off, I was able to focus her on a networking campaign. She had a great number of contacts, and with her skill-set and track record, it was reasonable that she would find something soon.

Unfortunately, Annie could not shake her negative attitude. It showed in how she carried herself and the bitterness she expressed toward her former firm. Her network did not expand. She felt sorry for herself and colleagues began to avoid her.

We decided to suspend her search and began working on recreating her identity independent of her career. Annie looked at how she was treating herself and learned to challenge her negative thinking and assumptions. She reflected on what was really meaningful to her and what kind of contribution she wanted to make. Rather than trying to fit herself into the box of whatever job she came across, she focused on writing her own ideal job from the inside out. We then rehearsed her story to make sure she was able to show her best self.

When she started networking again she got very different results, and the positive momentum snowballed. Each contact led to two or three more contacts, and people started brainstorming about how they could make a spot for her in their organization. She was soon able to pick between two different positions she had helped to create during the interview process. She still struggles at times with negative thinking and self-doubt. However, working at a job she loves helps her stay positive and gives her the opportunity to feel good about her value and impact.

Chapter 19

Tolerating Uncertainty
and Change

Lars was a VP of marketing for a Dutch chocolate company. He was forty years old and had two children with his wife, Lori. After helping his company grow across Europe for the past several years, Lars was asked to go to New York to head up the company's office there. Leading the sales force in New York was central to growing their U.S. business.

Lars felt a mix of excitement and fear. He had traveled extensively and spoke English fluently, but he had never lived overseas. Relocating his family meant significant personal disruption. As with any significant change, this also meant he had to deal with feelings of loss. He was losing contact with his friends and the comfort of a job he knew well and excelled at. Being away from the home office in Amsterdam meant being away from the center of power. He worried that he would be out of sight and out of mind when it came time for promotions. Though New York was an important center of the future, being sent there felt like being ostracized and losing control of his career.

Compounding his insecurity was the fact that his new role was ambiguous. Was he supposed to just manage the New York office or was he responsible for growing the U.S. region? Though he was head of the office, the different groups in New York (HR, product management, store operations and distribution) did not directly report to him. Each had a functional manager in Holland.

Lars's boss, Sharon, told him that his primary responsibility was for the sales function. However, the powerful COO of the company, Ted, told him he also needed to facilitate across functions and ensure the administrative aspects of the office ran smoothly. Neither Sharon nor Ted empathized with the level of uncertainty Lars was experiencing, and so they did not think about how they needed to communicate and support him.

Lars came to New York with a lot of ideas about how to run the office more effectively. He was impatient to make his mark and frustrated with the lack of clarity coming from Sharon and Ted. He was reluctant to confront Sharon and Ted because he was already feeling isolated and did not want to create any conflict or risk getting them angry.

Rather than listening to the core of what he was feeling, his first impulse when he felt anxiety or frustration was to act. He thought that at least if he was doing something, he would feel better and maybe change the situation. Distracting himself by plunging into action made him run fast in all directions. He took on administrative work instead of delegating because waiting to see how someone else would do it increased his anxiety. Rather than risk work wouldn't be up to his standards, doing it himself ensured he wouldn't have to deal with the uncertainty. He checked every invoice from his office manager and questioned why FedEx packages had been shipped express instead of the cheaper two-day option. His staff started to complain to headquarters about Lars's bullying and controlling behavior.

Experiment: Softening Impatience and Frustration

My first objective in coaching Lars was to get him to tune in to what he was feeling and stay with it. Try this the next time you experience impatience or frustration:

- Focus on your breathing and take one or two mindful breaths to settle yourself.

- Come back to your feeling and decide if it is at a level where you can explore it.

- Bring your attention to the situation and what is causing you to feel blocked. See if you can look at both your role and the perspective of the other people involved.

- Come back to your feeling again and see how much of it has melted.

• Recognize your ability to soften what you are feeling and use insights you get to find a way through.

Impatience often goes with worrying how you are going to solve something quickly. You can plan a set of steps, but your anxiety may be pushing you to get them done prematurely so you can get closure. The need for closure can be a big problem when you are faced with uncertainty. The best way to develop patience is to practice pulling out of your thinking in order to stay with the process of your feelings.

◆ ◆ ◆

Lars had high hopes for how he could grow New York and the U.S. business. Hiring product development staff in New York was an obvious step if they were going to tailor chocolates for this market. There was some buzz back in Holland about this happening, but it was not clear when. Lars was also keen to manage this function directly. He felt this would give him the platform he needed to be recognized and get promoted.

As time went on and no changes were announced, Lars's hopes led to more frustration. He was living in expectations rather than reality. As we talked, Lars realized he was acting as if his life would start only after he reached a fantasy of perfection. The formula for this self-defeating mind-set was, "I will be happy if.... "[1] I asked Lars to focus instead on how he could be happy in his present situation, even though it was ambiguous and potentially uncomfortable.

Experiment: Distinguishing Control from Choice

Lars faced a universal paradox. While you do not have much control, you do have a significant number of choices. Lars could not dictate specific outcomes like getting promoted or being given more responsibility. However, he could choose between a number of options with regard to how he treated his team, his attitude, and what he was able to learn.

Lars started to accept that all the issues he faced managing his people were necessarily gray and complex. Lars began to think of his job as being a "garbage man" because he was always cleaning up messy problems. When he came to terms with this, he got a lot more tolerant of the constant stream of problems that came his way, none of which had neat solutions.

- Make a list of all the things in your life you *do not* have control over. Include things like your parents, where you were born, and everything you can think of.

- Make a second list of all the areas in your life where you have choices.

- Notice how focusing on your choices expands your sense of ownership over your experience, enlarges your ability to see possibilities, and changes your assumptions about what you can accomplish.[2]

◆ ◆ ◆

Before I began working with Lars, Sharon and Ted had given Lars some very direct feedback. They told him that his micromanaging and at times explosive outbursts of frustration were unacceptable, especially if he wanted to become an SVP. Lars worked diligently with me to develop greater self-awareness and control. Mindfulness training strengthened his ability to sit with feelings without reacting and to use the information to make decisions. His growing ability to tolerate uncertainty enabled him to stay open longer and take in more, and thus he was able to quickly learn new leadership skills.

Lars continued practicing in order to trust his inner process. As he thought about how to bring the whole New York team together, I explained that the next step was learning to trust a group process. Together we designed a team session where the New York function heads could talk about their vision for the U.S. business.

I asked the team to start their off-site with a few minutes of silence in order to reflect on their purpose for the next two days. The operations director looked at me as if I was an alien, but he went along. The session went very well and the operations director later joked with me that he almost had a coronary when I suggested the silence. **Tolerating silence is central to being able to listen.** Teams often feel the need to fill open space when a few moments to consider the last statement would be more productive.

Growing the U.S. business would mean bringing a great deal of change to the organization. Many new staff and salespeople would have to be hired and trained, and the current staff would have to change their roles. Some of the current staff did not have the capabilities needed for the new roles, and so they would either have to find new roles or leave the company. The team needed to anticipate and plan for the changes this growth initiative would involve.

Experiment: Helping Yourself and Your Team through Change

Death is the ultimate loss, and the emotional reactions to death provide a good model for understanding loss and change.[3] The outline below breaks down our typical emotional reactions to loss into four stages with the associated emotional and behavioral signs. Following the signs are responses that can help us let go of the stage and move on. Empathy and communication are the most powerful tools in the process of moving through the stages of change.

Denial

- *Signs:* Avoidance, apathy, and withdrawal.
- *Responses:* Communicate and support; refrain from confronting the person before he or she can hear you.

Anger, Depression, and Anxiety

- *Signs:* Blaming and complaining, low productivity, and illness.
- *Responses:* Listen, acknowledge feelings, give feedback to refocus the person on the job; avoid criticizing.

Disorientation

- *Signs:* Overpreparation, confusion, bargaining, and scattered energy.
- *Responses:* Focus on priorities and set short-term goals; provide encouragement for positive behavior.

Acceptance

- *Signs:* Commitment to team goals, optimism, collaboration, and productivity.

- *Responses:* Focus on long-term goals, validate understanding of plans; reward and celebrate team successes.

Use the following principles to create a plan to help your team through change:

1. Identify the stage you are in. Then identify the stage each of your team members is in.

2. Realize that as the team leader you will go through the stages faster than your people. You have access to information sooner and have a broader perspective on why the change makes sense.

3. Recognize that people get stuck in stages for a lot of reasons, but it is worse when they are faced with impatience, lack of acceptance or pressure to just get on with it. The key is to empathize with their emotional reactions to change, however odd or misguided they may appear.

4. Communicate the reasons for the change, and paint a clear picture of the future. We can give up the past more easily when we have a better future to look forward to.

5. Use the change as an opportunity to engage people and collectively create new ways of working. Make sure everyone has a role to play in helping make the transition happen and in the design of the end state.

6. Create a public plan that serves as a roadmap for the change process and helps people know what will happen at each step. Provide any information, training, and support team members will need to be successful in their new roles.

◆ ◆ ◆

After six months Lars felt he had made significant progress developing and leading the growth initiative. He went to Sharon for feedback. Lars was shocked and hurt that she was not convinced he had changed. Part of the problem was the distance. Sharon could not see how Lars operated on a day-to-day basis in New York. The other issue was that Sharon had formed a conclusion based on the early staff complaints, and it was easier to keep her view of Lars than entertain potentially contradictory information. Sharon's filters and prejudices reflected her own strategy for dealing with uncertainty given the amount of information she had coming at her each day.

I suggested it could help for me to interview his staff and peers in New York. They felt that he had, in fact, made a remarkable turnaround. He was no longer checking every invoice and expenditure. He was facilitating across functions even though he did not have control and had created a positive and collaborative atmosphere in the office. With Lars's approval I gave a summary of the feedback to Sharon. As it came from an objective third party, she was more able to take in the new information. Lars was also able to convince Sharon to come and spend a week in New York so she could see first hand what he was doing. Sharon's trip convinced her it was time to for Lars to lead a product development function in New York and time to promote him to SVP.

According to actress Mae West, too much of a good thing can be wonderful. When it comes to tolerating uncertainty, though, this is not always true. Too much uncertainty in relationships can lead to our being taken advantage of. A client recently told me the story of her marriage and divorce after twenty years to someone who was not the best partner for her. At some point you have to conclude if it is not working and call it quits. Overtoleration is usually based on stifling feelings that would be self-protective (e.g., anger or anxiety) rather than using the information they provide. It is also important to be clear that nonjudging in relationships does not mean abdicating responsibility. We still need to use our judgment (intellect, intuition, and feelings) to discriminate and make distinctions between people. We need to decide which candidate to hire, which employee deserves a bonus, and which relationships are healthy and unhealthy.

Ultimately, valuing uncertainty has to do with faith and trust. We can have faith in ourselves, our skills, and our instincts. We can trust in process and trust our network. If I don't have the answer, I can get advice from someone I respect. Faith in these things gives us confidence we can make it through difficult times and get to a positive outcome. We can also trust in something larger than ourselves, like life, spirit, or God. Trust in these dimensions provides a different level of confidence — that no matter what the outcome, we will be okay.

> Everything happens for a reason. In other words, there is a lesson in everything if we are available and open to it. I focus on staying present in the moment so I can do my best and learn from whatever happens. I have faith that it will be for the best no matter what the outcome is.
>
> — *Yvette Vargas, head of Talent and Diversity,*
> *UBS Wealth Management*

Chapter 20

Multitasking and Technology

Bryn started her career as a customer service operator in a call center. She was able to listen and solve customer problems quickly while new information and emails were continually coming across her screen. She was identified as a high potential and rotated to the sales desk. There too her ability to juggle helped her excel. When her company downsized, it collapsed a number of positions. The head of the call center, Jean, asked Bryn to head up the combined sales and customer support teams.

Bryn's new job was significantly more complex, and she felt increased pressure to get a lot done at once. Rather than think ahead or prioritize, though, when she sat down at her desk in the morning the first thing she did was wade through the emails that had accumulated overnight. When she tried to focus on longer-term projects she found it difficult not to look at the icon in the corner of her screen that told her she had a new email. Given how many messages she received, this meant she almost always had the little symbol calling her attention. So every minute or two she would stop what she was doing and check her email.

Her staff disengaged as Bryn took calls during one-on-one meetings and checked her PDA every few minutes. She couldn't help glancing at her screen while she was on conference calls and was embarrassed when Jean asked her a question and she wasn't paying attention. Jean suggested she turn off her screen and put her PDA away while she was in meetings. However, it was rewarding for Bryn to look at email. Each email meant that someone thought she was important, and so she wanted to read each one as soon as possible.

While multitasking was helpful in Bryn's previous roles, as a leader it was interfering. She could not develop her people or think about ways to improve her team's work because she was constantly switching tasks and allowing interruptions. She avoided making important decisions and felt safer transacting. Bryn readily acknowledged her struggle when Jean asked her if she was happy, and so Jean offered Bryn a seat back on the customer support desk. She now uses her strong service orientation to help customers, and she models for new hires how to succeed in the role.

Your heart beats without instruction, and you can breathe and digest your lunch simultaneously. Your lower brain centers take care of these activities quite well on their own. You can even walk and chew gum at the same time because your motor cortex has overlearned these behaviors. In order to learn or perform complex tasks, though, you need to engage regions in your brain's frontal lobes. These areas of your cortex perform a set of operations neuroscientists call your executive function.

Your executive function is your conscious choice-maker. It is how you exert self-control when you are so mad you want to hit someone but decide to walk around the block instead. Your executive function thinks ahead, makes plans, and decides what deserves attention. It filters distractions, for example, lowering the volume of the siren in the street so you can continue reading. Over time, mindfulness exercises can increase the thickness of areas of your frontal lobes along with the capacity of your executive function.[1] You can learn to concentrate for as long as you want and change focus to one task to another when you want. However, at any given moment, you have to work with a fixed quantity of attention and willpower.

When you multitask you are asking your executive function to switch rapidly between tasks. This is what a computer does when you ask it to surf the web while calculating an Excel spreadsheet and simultaneously play a podcast in the background. The microprocessor handles this by time-sharing. It does a little bit of work on each task and keeps switching back and forth rapidly to keep all of them moving. Unfortunately, when you try to do the same thing, you have to spend a lot of time figuring out where you were before you switched tasks in order to get back on track. Working this way ends up taking a lot longer and creating a lot more errors. You have to remind yourself not to overestimate your ability to multitask in order to avoid overload.

Experiment: Mindful Consumption

The irony is that we now have access to a wealth of information, but we are less able to use it because there is too much. Given the limited capacity of our brains, stretching our attention to take more in means we learn and remember less. Technology has produced an incredible ease of communication and availability of information. This makes it even more vital that we learn to sort, sift, and synthesize what comes at us. We also need to limit what we deal with.

Consider all the sources of information you consume. How much information do you want to voluntarily take in each day? How much is healthy? How much is unhealthy?

- Think about your complete diet of magazines, newspapers, snail mail, email, TV programs, and radio shows.

- How much time do you spend absorbing information rather than reflecting on, processing, and creating information?

- Are you trying to digest more than is realistic?

- What is your balance of positive and negative information?

- What changes can you easily make in your diet without feeling deprived?

- Can you cancel some of your magazine subscriptions and cable TV channels?

- How many email accounts do you need?

◆ ◆ ◆

We have very sophisticated technology but are struggling even more with communication. Email and texting have made miscommunication rampant because they remove the interpersonal cues we depend on to decode information. It is challenging to decipher text without the 70 percent context we get from nonverbal cues. At least on the phone we can use the tone and music of the other person's voice to help us.

A large bank referred an executive to me because of the email war she had started. She was head of service and was frustrated with the support her clients received from operations. Rather than picking up her phone, her instinct was to blast her operations colleagues via email (cc-ing their bosses and peers of course). Though she was an intensely rational person, her fighter instinct was strong, and she could easily be provoked by any perceived violation of her sense of fairness. I helped her become more aware of her triggers and coached her on assertiveness and win/win negotiations. She learned to have direct conversations with her colleagues and thus avoided what was about to be a career-limiting maneuver.

Humor translates via email as poorly as anger. I have had more than one client sorry they sent a hilarious email to everyone in the company. There is always at least one person who chooses to be offended. These clients now use their draft folders and sleep on emails before hitting send. Try to put yourself in your readers' shoes and remember they do not know the context that you do. Then read your email critically to test if it will make sense to them. Also try reading emails out loud to increase your perspective and to get greater objectivity.

Experiment: Email and Communication Breaks

The colors and movement of TV and PDA screens are incredibly seductive, and we easily become addicted.[2] Many of my clients receive hundreds of emails each day, to say nothing of texts and instant messages. With all these distractions, companies are starting to realize there is a problem getting work done. Intel tried a pilot program of email-free Fridays in one department. At first the employees liked it and recommended the practice be expanded, but ultimately they couldn't stick with it. The employees decided email was too essential to part with for even a day.

One of my clients sponsored a women's leadership program and asked me to speak about resilience. Many of the women attending were entrepreneurs with demanding jobs who also took lead roles at home with child care. When we started talking about email, it was clear that it was a large source of aggravation. I was inspired by the number of women who made commitments to set firm boundaries on email. Many decided they would not look at email after they got home, and many others declared they would not check email on weekends.

- How long can you go before you have to check your email? Do you look at email on your PDA while you are walking down the street? Decide how often it really makes sense to check during the day at home and on weekends. The less you check, the more you can think.

- Are you always available and connected? Do you feel you have to respond immediately when a message comes in? You can train colleagues and friends not to expect instantaneous responses to email and voicemail. Tell them you will respond within twenty-four hours unless it is an emergency. Just because email comes at the speed of light doesn't mean you have to respond that quickly.

◆ ◆ ◆

Technology's distractions and interruptions are not all bad. Especially if we are engaged in relatively routine and simple tasks, interruptions can provide us with helpful new information and feedback. If the new information is challenging enough it can wake us up and provoke new insights. It can lead us to reexamine our assumptions and perspective and thus to change direction.[3] Technology is also a powerful force for social change. Oppressive regimes cannot control information and dialogue as easily as the texting crowds in the Arab Spring Revolution proved. Moreover, the Internet is breaking down barriers between cultures and starting to connect us as a global community. Technology can thus be very positive, but we must be careful to understand our capacity to manage it.

A man's got to know his own limitations.

—*Dirty Harry*

Chapter 21

Prioritization
and Time Management

There is so much you want to do, and you get advice from all corners about how to lead a healthy life.

> *How do you floss regularly, eat eight servings of fruit and vegetables a day, drink lots of water, exercise at least thirty minutes at least three times a week, attend religious services regularly, belong to groups that matter to you and attend their meetings, keep up with your friends, not neglect your outside interests, work your job, raise your kids, do the laundry, pay taxes, have sex at least once a week, deal with the pressure of relentless uncertainty, and change the oil in your car every three thousand miles without possessing the powers of a miracle maker?* — Edward Hallowell

With all these things on your list, it is understandable that you would complain about not having enough time. Physicists argue, though, that **time is a psychological construction and not a physical dimension of the universe.**[1] This may sound strange, but you can experience this in a number of ways. When you travel to the Caribbean, where there are fewer time-saving devices, time paradoxically slows down. Locals call it "Island Time." A forty-minute trance during self-hypnosis can seem to last five minutes. In meditation, when you focus completely in the present, the past and future dissolve. Time stops.

You cannot manage time when you think of it as an inexorably marching clock. The perspective that there is never enough time creates a great deal of stress. The endless series of "have-to" items on your list can lead you to feel anxious, hopeless, and overwhelmed. When you manage yourself and your attention, however, time becomes more malleable and manageable. The key is to focus on self-management rather than time management.[2] Practicing self-management is about taking responsibility rather than hiding behind excuses like, "There just isn't enough time."

Stan was the chief procurement officer for a global consumer products company with over a hundred thousand employees. He felt a great deal of weight on his shoulders and was always running to keep up. He realized he could become negative, self-critical, and task-focused.

Stan started asking the fundamental self-management question: "What is the most important thing to do right now?" Asking this helped him step back and think about where he was running. However, as he revved up through the day, it became difficult to remember to ask this question. He put a note on his computer telling him to take a breath and a picture of his favorite vacation spot on his desk. Unfortunately, he was on the go so much he was seldom sitting at his desk. He decided to take a breath every time he shook someone's hand.

This helped Stan a great deal, because he was often shaking hands, but it was still extremely difficult for him to remember to bring attention to his intention. We discussed cultivating mindfulness and concentration as a longer-term strategy. He began with five minutes of meditation three times a week. Just this amount helped him pull out of the stream of his habits and constant activity to reflect and refocus. Stan was able to regularly ask "What now?" as well as the important follow-up, "What is the full range of my choices?" Looking at the full range of his available options and choices enabled him to more effectively prioritize.

Stan started to feel like he was pulling his head above water and he started to enjoy his work more. He was running less and focusing on the most value-added activities. I asked him to add one final question: "What are the consequences of pursuing this goal or activity?" This question linked his choices with his longer-term purpose. It also made him anticipate the unintended political and organizational consequences of what he was doing.

Experiment: Building a Self-Management Plan

All the little tasks and errands that need to get done can easily consume you and cause you to miss the most important things. Pick one or two items from the checklist below that could help you manage yourself through your load of tasks. Some may appear obvious on the surface, but most are difficult to put into practice. The list includes some suggestions and reminders from previous chapters.

SELF-MANAGEMENT/ TIME MANAGEMENT CHECKLIST

I. Choices

Remind yourself to regularly ask:

    A. "What is the most important thing to do right now?"

    B. "What is the full range of my choices?"

    C. "What are the consequences of pursuing this goal or activity?"

II. Task Management

    A. Chunking

        1. Divide large tasks into manageable pieces.

        2. If you feel overwhelmed or are procrastinating, tackle the easiest piece first to build momentum.

        3. Concentrate on only one thing at a time.

        4. Apply the 80/20 rule (80 percent of the value is usually in 20 percent of the time):

            a. Start with the most profitable part.

            b. Analyze the value of spending another minute on a particular item.

            c. Cut off nonproductive activities as quickly as possible.

            d. Be aware of perfectionism; let go of less critical details.

    B. Scheduling

        1. Block out time to concentrate on high priority items.

        2. Select the best time of day for the type of work required.

3. Reserve at least one hour a day of uncommitted time.

4. If you cannot avoid back-to-back meetings, begin to wrap up each ten minutes early so you have at least five minutes to get ready for the next meeting.

5. Schedule regular short breaks to allow you to process what you have just done.

C. Focusing

1. Keep a readily visible reminder of your top priority tasks.

2. Think about how each small task you are doing is connected to your longer-term goals.

3. Make a note to yourself of where you are and the next step before you allow interruptions.

4. Balance your time between urgent/short-term tasks and important/long-term projects and objectives.

5. When you think of something you want to do, quickly get it off your mind and onto a consolidated set of lists (Shopping, Work To Do's, etc.) so it doesn't take up mindshare and distract you.

III. Self-Discipline

A. Paperwork

1. Handle pieces of paper only once. Touch them when you are ready to act on them.

2. Use "Keep the ball in the other person's court" to keep paper moving meaningfully.

3. Sort reading material into two stacks: "Want to Read" and "Read if Time." Regularly throw out items that collect in the "Read if Time" pile. If you find you never get to read these, don't bother saving them in the first place.

4. Have short tasks (sorting mail) handy for when you may be waiting (at the doctor's office).

B. Meetings and Phone Calls

   1. State the purpose early and bring meetings back when they get off track.

   2. If you are not sure what the agenda is, ask.

   3. Minimize distractions that keep you from being present.

   4. When you have accomplished the purpose, ask if it is okay to end early.

   5. Recognize when colleagues are stopping by to take a break and relax; don't be afraid to say so if this is not a good time.

   6. Put a "busy thinking" sign on your door or cube when you don't want interruptions.

C. Delegation

   1. Recognize tendencies to "just do it yourself" and reflect on root causes.

   2. Review your To-Do list and put a "D" next to any item you can delegate, especially if it would develop your people.

   3. Use a separate delegation list to track assigned tasks and delivery dates.

   4. Get your assistant to manage you. Brainstorm with him about how he can help focus you, protect your time, and take things off your plate.

   5. Expect work you give to direct reports and colleagues to be completed on time; explain the consequences when it is not.

   6. If you feel too much work is being delegated to you, ask your boss to help you prioritize. Balance being supportive with pushing back so you can avoid overcommitment.

IV. Revising Rhythms

A. Pacing

   1. Monitor how fast you move during different activities.

   2. What is your natural pace or rhythm?

3. Choose the most effective pace for different activities.

4. What pace allows you to be the most present for important conversations?

5. Establish rituals that help you change pace when you stop working and go home. Capitalize on the effect of natural rhythms (rocking chairs, ocean waves) as well as changing scenery (changing your clothes, going outside).

B. Stopping and Reflecting

1. Make time for reflecting and relaxing. Challenge the belief that it is a waste of time if you are not always doing something.

2. Reflect on and modify your plan:

   a. How successful are you at making choices, task management, self-discipline, and pacing?

   b. What you are learning?

   c. What changes do you want to make to your self-management plan?

◆ ◆ ◆

Jerry was the CFO of a division of a Fortune 500 manufacturing company. At thirty he was a rising star with lots of ambition, intellect, and commitment. His boss, Mike, considered several stretch assignments but hesitated because of Jerry's immaturity and lack of patience, focus, and discipline. Mike asked me to coach Jerry to become more aware of his impact and to develop his ability to think strategically and build relationships with a broad set of constituents. There was also a concern about burnout. While Jerry had prodigious energy, he never said "no." He worked all hours of the day and night, and seldom took any time off.

Jerry needed to learn to focus, self-monitor, and stop the action. His day was filled with meetings and then he worked all night to catch up on the accumulated follow-up tasks. He allowed his people to delegate upward. They asked him to make decisions for them and solve their problems. We discussed his values and he wrote: "My highest priorities are cultivating deep relationships with my team and protecting my thinking time." To do this he realized he would need to set limits — on distractions, on interruptions, and with his people.

Jerry was a very nice guy. Too nice. The implication of his priorities was that he would need to be more ruthless (without being nasty). He started practicing saying "no" to people, which was at first very difficult but ultimately grew his team's ability to make decisions for themselves. Saying "no" also meant not accepting meeting invitations when he was not really needed. If he was meeting with someone, that person needed to be the most important at that moment. Phone calls could wait. If he was on the phone with someone, he would not look at emails. They could wait. Having this clear hierarchy of priorities ensured he stayed present and maintained the clarity of his thinking.

Having more time to think and prepare helped Jerry become more analytical and disciplined. Preparation also helped him reign in his enthusiasm and negotiate and influence more objectively. He learned to tune in to interpersonal cues and gauge his impact. Tuning in to his gut helped him know when he needed a break and when to stop working. Jerry started the ritual of taking a long weekend once a month, and then added a full week off twice a year.

Once Jerry had his team and volume of work under control he was ready to start focusing outward. He targeted seven key constituents and actively worked to build greater trust, mutual support, and value. Reflection on the market helped him articulate a vision, and reflection on his purpose helped him clarify his career goals. After eighteen months Mike promoted Jerry, and he is now heading up a successful start-up business for the company.

Experiment: Avoiding Overcommitment — Just Say "No"

Most of us have a strong need to be liked and to avoid conflict. Thus we have difficulty saying "no" and facing conflict. Saying "yes" to what everyone else wants gets us into the habit of over-toleration and over-commitment.

- Look for opportunities to establish boundaries and say "no."

- Trust this will improve rather than interfere with your relationships. You may find this results in some natural "weeding" as you let go of some relationships that are not mutually supportive.

- The flip side of learning to set limits is learning to accept limits when they are set with you. Giving people who live and work with you the space to set their own boundaries further strengthens your relationships and develops your patience and understanding.

◆ ◆ ◆

Experiment: Aligning Tasks and Purpose

- Make a short list of the big To-Do's in your life — the major things you are trying to accomplish, not the micro tasks.

- Now go back to the set of values and the purpose you created in the earlier experiments on clarifying values (p. 52) and envisioning purpose (p. 54).

- Reflect on whether you are prioritizing your To-Do list in alignment with values and purpose, and if there are any changes you would make.

- What is one thing you could give up? Think about whether making a hard choice to simplify and let go of something unessential could free you up to focus on what you care most about.

◆ ◆ ◆

Part IV

Conclusions
and Implications

You should now have enough ideas about possible activities, experiments, and skills to complete your leadership development plan. This plan will enable you to keep your learning on target and to keep up your momentum. The first chapter in this section provides a framework to set goals and make sure your plan is solid. With your individual development launched, we can look at bigger picture issues and the context in which you work.

The second chapter applies the principles of goal-setting to organizations. One of the principal imperatives of leadership is focusing teams and organizations. This means managing everyone's attention. As team members, we also need to recognize the ways our organization's focus affects our own. Goals can be helpful in focusing attention, but they can also be dangerous.

In the last chapter I widen our focus as far as possible. I temporarily suspend questions of individual and organizational effectiveness to look at questions of purpose and the nature of attention. We can use attention as a tool, but we also need to examine what attention is and how it relates to who we are. Understanding who we are is vital if we are going to create a vision for the future and the next generation of leaders.

Chapter 22

Goal-Setting and Development Planning

Tami was high energy, confident, ambitious, and results-oriented. She had recently joined a large financial services organization which had a very relationship- and consensus-oriented culture. Her previous company was more direct and hard-driving, which fit her style. Tami's boss, Katherine, knew this would make Tami's integration a challenge. Her success depended on her adjusting her approach and developing her team so she could drive a difficult global project.

It is never entirely clear when I begin a coaching process how much my clients own the feedback that have been given. The first good measure of this comes in the development plan. I was hopeful as Tami's plan came together. It hit all the key themes and communicated that she was taking responsibility for her behavior. I met with Tami and Katherine to review the plan and make sure we were all aligned. There were no surprises, just lots of positive feedback and encouragement from Katherine.

Clear goals focus effort and attention. They help you know where you are headed and keep organizations aligned. The most effective leaders communicate regularly about their goals. This mobilizes their people's energy and keeps everyone moving in the same direction.[1]

Goals can also be a double-edged sword. If you hold on to them too tightly they can narrow your vision and blind you to alternatives along the way. Becoming consumed by goals and wanting to win too badly decreases your openness to corrective feedback and your willingness to change. As a result, you can miss opportunities for new products, new businesses, and new learning.

Goals are useful so you know the ultimate target, but not as the ongoing focus. Goals help us as a reference point, a mark that tells us if we are on track. It is a fine line, though, between checking with the goal, and evaluating yourself against the goal. When you compare your position to the goal, you remind yourself of how you are not there yet. You take yourself out of the process and have the potential to get tense, impatient, and self-critical.

You reach goals more quickly when you concentrate on what you are doing now to move yourself forward, i.e., when you focus on the process rather than on outcomes. You set goals because you think they will make you happy. Then all along the way you say, "I will be happy when I reach my goal." When you finally arrive you find there is just a short-term emotional payoff. You need to retrain yourself not to take the fun out of the process or treat the means to the end as a nuisance. Mindfulness increases goal achievement because it teaches you to enjoy and stay with the process.

Experiment: Completing Your Development Plan

Return to the development plan you began drafting in the first chapter. Think about the experiments you tried in each subsequent chapter and add the ones that resonated for you.

A simple outline can work well for your plan, or you can use a spreadsheet format like Tami's (below). Your plan need not have all the following sections, and you can add other useful ones like "timeframe/schedule" and "strengths to leverage."

1. *Objectives:* what you want to accomplish

2. *Strategies:* competencies you want to develop

3. *Tactics:* specific skills you want to develop and behaviors you want to target within each strategy

4. *Expected Results:* how you will measure progress

A good way to make sure your action plan is rigorous is to apply Drucker's SMART guidelines, which subsequently became SMARTER.[2]

• *Specific:* When you commit to specific and actionable goals, it leads you to perform better than if you simply intend to do your best.[3]

"Work on becoming a better team player" is a vague wish. Tami's "Tune in to peers' goals and expectations in order to support their agendas" is specific and actionable.

- *Measurable:* The "Expected Results" column in Tami's plan ensures she has a way to assess if her plan is successful.
- *Achievable:* Tami's "Create a focused business plan" is a realistic short-term goal that can build positive momentum.
- *Relevant:* Tami's "Develop my vision" is an activity that makes sense for her role and will help the organization reach its objectives.
- *Time-bound:* If you know when you are planning to do something (or by when something needs to be done) there is a greater likelihood it will happen on schedule.
- *Extending:* "Delivering the global business services project" is an ambitious goal with the potential to extend Tami's capabilities. Setting aspirational goals can inspire you to become and achieve more than you thought possible. A "stretch objective" extends your capabilities and makes you use your imagination and energy to reach it. However, goals that are too aggressive may feel overwhelming and cause you to give up because they seem too far out of reach. Goals need to balance being extending and achievable.
- *Rewarding:* "Maintaining balance" and "Increased recognition and exposure" were rewarding for Tami. The process of working toward your goals should be enjoyable in itself. Find ways to monitor progress and reward yourself for moving in the right direction, not just for achieving perfect outcomes.

Also consider these dimensions:

- *Anticipation:* Think about what can go wrong and potential obstacles; plan for contingencies.
- *Resources:* Consider what help and resources you need to be successful. Engage key constituents early on and consider adding a relationship map to your plan (see chapter 14).
- *Environment:* Design and organize your workspace so you are comfortable and able to focus. Make sure your role is a good fit for your

strengths, interests and values. If you are unhappy in your job, include a career management section in your plan to get you to a better place.

- *Habits:* Use rituals and positive, reinforcing routines to help you develop self-discipline.

- *Patience:* Be patient with yourself and your development. Changing behavior takes time and does not occur without self-acceptance.

It can be hard to write a development plan because the focus tends to be negative, i.e., on things you are not good at and thus are uncomfortable facing. It is doubly hard to brainstorm tactics on your development areas because this is generally where you have blind spots. The plan also becomes a public commitment, which can be scary. Will you be able to accomplish this goal? Do you really want to change this behavior?

You can address some of these challenges by including "strengths to leverage" in your plan. For example, if you are terrible at organizing, but good at delegating, you can plan to delegate paperwork and filing to people on your team. You can also make development planning easier by engaging other people to coach you. The first time I tried writing a plan I stared hopelessly at a blank sheet of paper and then gave up. I finally sat down with a colleague who offered to help. Within a few minutes of brainstorming we had several actionable ideas. I was then able to add new tactics and flesh out my plan.

◆ ◆ ◆

After six months of coaching Tami, Katherine asked to meet with me. The feedback was that Tami's people loved her. She had recruited a strong team, advocated for them effectively, and built a great deal of loyalty. After an initial period when she appeared to have moderated her approach, though, Tami's peers and clients were beginning to complain. They saw her as headstrong, not listening, and pushing her project too fast. It was over budget and her clients were starting to worry that she was overselling and overcommitting. Katherine saw Tami trying to go it on her own without looping Katherine in. Tami had a high need for autonomy and would not consistently communicate about what she was doing.

ACTION PLAN —TAMI

DATE

Objectives:

✓ Design and deliver global business services project
✓ Increase senior management confidence in my leadership
✓ Enhance sense of well being & satisfaction

Strategies	Tactics	Expected Results
Develop influencing skills	Expand relationship-building and communication efforts. ♦ Create calendar for meetings to apprise senior management of goals and results. ♦ Develop relationship matrix including external networking channels. ♦ Identify key relationships that would benefit from strengthening and look for ways to add value for each. ♦ Make sure to listen and validate understanding. Flex to the culture ♦ Practice Win/Win negotiating. ♦ Adjust my approach in meetings. Be aware of projecting over-confidence/impatience. ♦ Work to understand current culture at the same time as promoting change. ♦ Anticipate risks & be ready to respond to concerns.	✓ Improved efficiency of communications ✓ Better input and feedback ✓ Increased recognition and exposure within firm ✓ More culturally acceptable plan for moving forward ✓ Stronger relationships and network both inside and outside the firm ✓ More win/win outcomes

Maximize impact

Gain consensus on strategic direction

- Identify areas where I can add value.
- Develop and actively communicate my vision.
- Create focused business plan and syndicate through network.
- Tune in to peers' goals and expectations in order to support their agendas.

✓ confidence in me as a leader
✓ Increased involvement at senior levels
✓ Be allowed to innovate
✓ Greater partnering with colleagues
✓ Expanded skills
✓ Smooth organizational succession

Develop team

- Ensure realistic development plans exist
- Increase positive and constructive feedback (formal and informal)
- Schedule regular coaching for team members on skills and careers
- Create viable succession plan and validate with superior
- Stretch key individuals to permit greater delegation.
- Conduct team-building off site/strategy session

Maintain balance

- Set boundaries on work; clarify availability with peers and team.
- Adopt regular telecommuting schedule.
- Work out more regularly (at least twice/week).
- Pay more attention to what I eat and its impact on my mood.
- Expand involvement in diversity and community outreach initiatives.

✓ Greater time for strategic thinking
✓ Greater personal satisfaction
✓ More energy/endurance

After a series of tough conversations, Tami and Katherine agreed it would be best for Tami to leave the organization. She had a good plan, but she had gone through the motions and her commitment to change was half-hearted. Tami is now working in a company whose competitive culture is a better fit for her style.

Many organizations require employees to write yearly objectives and development plans as part of their performance management process. Unfortunately, there is little attention paid to training managers and employees on how to write these effectively. The result is that most plans are more about performance than development. "Grow revenues by 10 percent" is simple and concrete. How to develop employees to achieve this goal is a lot more complex. As a result, development plans can become check-the-box activities. Employees end up filling in one or two items on the order of "Read a book" or "Take a class." More meaningful would be "Look for new project assignments and roles," but it is the rare organization that encourages job rotations.

Performance appraisals can be a challenge because leaders don't distinguish between performers. They evaluate production levels (the what) but not the skills people need to produce (the how). Once they take time for this, leaders also need more courage to give direct feedback so people know how to improve.

— *Neal Wendel, Managing Director,*
Human Resources, Credit Suisse

Performance reviews become something we dread. We get to know our team members well, and our familiarity and personal relationships make it harder to deliver feedback that we anticipate may not be well received. Moreover, the issues that block learning are often based on dysfunctional self-perceptions, beliefs, and habits that have gone unexamined. Beliefs like, "I will never be a good presenter because I get nervous in large groups" provide a measure of psychological security and may be central to our concept of ourselves.[4] We shy away from giving feedback that could challenge these negative assumptions and make our colleagues uncomfortable.

So how do you get the courage you need to give difficult feedback? You need to believe in the fundamental capacity of people to transform themselves in the context of support. I am continually reminded that people's egos are more sensitive than I would like to believe. Paradoxically, though, along with that fragility, people are also stronger and more resilient than we often give them credit for.

A central obstacle to individual development planning is our organization's goal-setting processes. Organizations spend a great deal of time and money crafting strategic plans and long-range goals. These goals are then cascaded down the organization, with each employee picking up pieces of their boss's goal in their individual plans. Performance goals that are rolled out top-down like this are less motivating. The organization focuses employees on what they want accomplished to the exclusion of what employees could learn. Development plans become the least emphasized part of the process, and so often do not integrate performance with personal development goals. The alternative is a participative goal-setting approach. While not impossible, this can be a formidable challenge in a large organization.

Chapter 23

Organizational Goals and Focus

Julian (or Jule as he was called) was a lawyer and accountant for most of his career. When I met him he was heading up administration and finance for the animal health division of a global pharmaceutical company. I coached him for nine months, after which he was promoted to run the division. The animal health division was a small part of his company, which was primarily devoted to human pharmaceuticals and personal care products. This gave Jule's division greater autonomy, but it also meant support and funding could at times be a challenge.

I had initially coached Jule to clarify his priorities and build his leadership skills. Now he needed to broaden his attention to set goals for his whole organization. This meant he had to shift his focus along two leadership MindShifts.

Personal Accountability . . . . **Organizational Accountability**
Monitoring your own work processes,   Measuring the organization's success
deadlines and goals   (profit, efficiency, quality, service);
     allocating and brokering resources

———————————————————————————————→

Task Analysis . . . . **Market Analysis**
Problem-solving the best way to   Deciding what business to be in, a vision
accomplish a task   for where it should go, and strategies
     to get there

———————————————————————————————→

Jule and I discussed a five-step process to set and implement his organization's goals:

1. *Participative goal-setting:* soliciting employee involvement in establishing goals.

2. *Communication:* articulating goals and validating understanding.

3. *Execution:* planning and implementing effective strategies and processes.

4. *Accounting:* setting up appropriate measures to keep track of progress toward goals.

5. *Reflection:* periodically reviewing results and modifying processes.

1 and 2. Participative Goal-Setting and Communication

Many hierarchical organizations don't promote reflection or solicit input into organizational goals because it can threaten the status quo. In such companies you may be paid for your creative intellect, but then you are really expected to do what your boss tells you. This can get worse the higher you go. Often in these organizations the CEO's word is taken as a commandment. A single offhand comment sends armies scurrying to implement what they think he wants. This can waste hours of time and energy that could have been saved by asking a single clarifying question. We need to have the courage to speak up and question the nature of the authority structures where we work. Open conversations are vital for our own health as well as the health of our organizations.

Participative goal-setting is the best way to align and engage an entire workforce's attention, energy, and effort. In Jule's organization, though, this would mean soliciting input from thousands of employees, which he felt would be unwieldy. As a compromise, he decided to gather input primarily from his customer-facing employees. For the rest of the process he would rely on top-down goal-setting, knowing this meant he would have to work harder to communicate the final goals in a way that would get people on board.

Jule asked his heads of new business development, marketing, and sales to conduct a market analysis. He wanted to know which business opportunities his organization was well positioned to go after. When the initial work was done, he planned to have his human resource function help determine if he had the necessary talent to go after these opportunities.

I facilitated an off-site session for Jule's top team where we looked at the information his people had gathered. We used a consensus decision-making process to agree on an overall mission and set five strategic priorities for the business. Their mission was to become the leader in pharmaceutical products to veterinarians across the world. Their strategic priorities were:

- Expanding their sales force to give them greater reach in emerging economies such as China and India

- Developing at least two new drugs for the fast-growing oncology market

- Creating a supportive work environment that would attract, retain, and develop top talent

- Launching a quality and service initiative to improve customers' confidence in their products and the support they would receive

- Conducting a review of their processes and organizational structure to reduce inefficiencies by at least $2 million per year

Jule was pleased with the outcome of the off-site. His team was charged up and the goals aligned with Jule's personal values around service and employee development. The goals were also succinct. At the off-site we created a one-page "strategic pillars" document to outline them along with the key initial tactics supporting each. This would make the goals easy to communicate across the organization.

Jule hesitated when it came time to share the strategic pillars with all his employees. His delay made me concerned about a number of potential negative consequences and so met with him to talk it through. Not being transparent about the goals and the process that led to them could allow employees to make negative assumptions about the state and direction of the business. I asked Jule to think about some of the common concerns that hold leaders back from communicating openly:

- Communicating goals will mean relinquishing control.
- I need complete clarity before communicating.
- I will be second-guessed about choosing these goals.

- I could be criticized if we don't reach these goals.

- I will not be able to answer employees' questions about why I chose these goals.

Jule realized that his concern was about being held accountable for success. He was not concerned about his bosses in the parent company. He had no choice but to show them his goals. However, he realized that it was important to him that his employees saw him as successful, and it would be potentially embarrassing to publish goals and then not meet them. Reflecting on this concern made it less potent, and Jule realized that not publishing the goals was contrary to his objective of creating a supportive work environment.

3. Execution

As an accountant, Jule knew he needed disciplined processes to implement his goals. His organization already had well-defined processes to ensure product specifications fell within narrow tolerances. He had project management specialists in a number of functions like R&D, as well as organizational development facilitators in the HR department. He would need these professionals to get thousands of employees moving in the same direction to address his five strategic priorities and to help teams through the emotional and logistical challenges of change.

I cautioned Jule not to overdo process in his effort to scale his initiatives across his organization. His culture had a growing entrepreneurial spirit. Too much process for control and standardization could add bureaucracy and stifle independent initiative. His strategic priorities made sense now. But as markets and competitors changed direction, he needed to be able to adjust, and too much consistency and predictability could get in his way.

Jule understood the danger. He had seen multiple systemic processes like Six Sigma and Total Quality Management end up focusing employees so much on efficiency that they stopped innovating. He did not want to see his organization so attached to the security of following processes that they lost sight of the goal. An obvious option was to hire a consulting firm like Accenture or Deloitte to help drive toward his $2 million cost-savings target with new technology and a tightly orchestrated process. However, Jule felt his organization would respond better to change driven from within, by people who knew the culture and could continue the momentum beyond the confines of a typical consulting contract.

Jule brought his HR team together. They were enthusiastic about the opportunity to help bring change and support the strategic priorities. However, other than three or four organizational development facilitators, they did not feel they had the necessary skills. Jule asked if they wanted to skill up in consulting, coaching, and facilitation skills. They could pick the vendor; he would pick up the tab. They jumped at the chance.

4. Accounting

Jule's next task was to figure out how to assess progress. The obvious measures included:

- How much product did we sell?
- What was our gross revenue?
- What were our expenses?
- What was our profit?

These measures would focus employees' attention, but would orient people to quantity rather than quality. They would tell him little about the true health of the business and would probably not inspire many people. Jule wanted to find measures that could assess the development of a supportive work environment. He also wanted to assess quality differently. He wanted to assess quality closer to the way we evaluate a gift we are thinking about buying for a friend — by using an intuitive felt sense. This was a challenge for an organization used to assessing quality only with carefully calibrated lab instruments.

Jule reasoned that if he could find a way to get employees to focus on quality and service their work could become a craft they could care deeply about. The dedication to craftsmanship and standards has a tremendous ability to inspire dedication and drive high performance teamwork.[1] Jule knew he could not institute measures top down, so he asked each function to suggest a meaningful scorecard. The process of investigating potential quality and service measures became a key part of the change effort that engaged a great number of employees. It was not just manufacturing that was responsible for quality. Staff functions like finance and procurement also came up with quality and service measures to ensure they were meeting their internal customer's expectations.

The HR department adapted the year-end employee performance appraisal process so that the new quality and service measures joined the traditional concrete production and financial targets. The new appraisal process included assessments of quality, teamwork, leadership behaviors, talent development, service to customers, and creativity. This had another unanticipated effect. The HR department started to record fewer employee relations and ethical issues as people were no longer incentivized to take the shortest route to performance goals.

Jule realized the timing of measurement was also important. Reviewing success against goals could not be a daily event. The parent company had just started posting its stock price on monitors in building lobbies and elevators. Jule asked if he could indefinitely postpone these facilities improvements and use the money for employee recognition instead. He did not want employees feeling good or bad about their work each day as the numbers went up and down based on a market they had no influence on. His parent company insisted on quarterly financial reports even though the business cycles he faced were on much longer time frames. He worked with his CFO to create these, but he did not want the rest of his leaders focused on making the numbers line up every three months. He wanted them looking at how to grow the business over the long term.

Jule thought carefully about the deadlines he set. This was especially relevant for his goal of developing two new oncology drugs. He wanted to create a sense of urgency in the R&D pipeline without stifling exploration and discovery. He recognized that deadlines are extraordinary focusing mechanisms and thus key levers. **The word "deadline" itself connotes catastrophe: miss the deadline and you die.** Though it was never really life or death, giving his people deadlines would give goals extra power. He carefully negotiated some deadlines with his R&D head and coached her to be selective in setting corresponding deadlines within her organization.

5. Reflection

Jule wanted his employees to become more reflective, independent thinkers. When he met with each of his top team he would ask them to review their process, not just their progress toward goals. Teams were encouraged to conduct regular reviews of how well they were working together. Projects would conclude with "after-action reviews" similar to what the military uses to make sure there are lessons learned from every engagement.

Jule's organization was used to conducting an annual employee survey. Jule was keen to continue this given the research connecting employee engagement with lower turnover and higher profits. Jule asked his HR team to take a fresh look at the survey in light of the new strategic priorities. The HR team decided to add a number of new items including:

- Are internal and external customers satisfied or do they want something different?
- What additional skill sets do we need?
- What are our culture's assumptions and values?
- Are these values positively influencing our employees' attention, thinking and behavior?
- Is our culture based on trust?
- Can our culture attract the best talent?
- How is power distributed in our organization?

Given his earlier hesitancy about communicating transparently, I cautioned Jule that he needed to be prepared to report all of the survey results back to employees. He also needed to be prepared to act on what he heard or risk employees feeling the process was insincere. Jule had invested a great deal in his employees feeling cared about and he did not want to undermine that.

The survey results at the end of the year confirmed that Jule had transformed his culture. His parent company didn't really care. Their goal was for him to produce goods and services and to make a profit, which he was doing. However, he was determined not to let the profit motive swamp customer and employee needs. Being decent to employees was not just a personal value; it was a driver of employee engagement and thus a driver of business success.

When I last talked to Jule he was engaging his organization in a dialogue about corporate social responsibility. This would be an effort to serve not only the needs of employees and customers, but also of the community and the environment. A series of conversations was going on across the organization about the value of investing in sustainable business practices and attempts to reduce their environmental footprint. Jule was taking another step beyond shareholder return and attempting to shift his organization even further away from a short-term survival mentality to long-term service mentality. Given the values of his employees, and especially the younger generation, Jule understood this would be more than altruistic. Sustainable business practices could reduce his operating costs while creating more engaged and productive employees.

Experiment: Organizational Goal-Setting

Take your organization through this five-step process to set and implement an important goal. Rather than going for whole-scale organizational transformation, start with a relatively narrow objective, such as reducing the level of stress in your organization. As you engage your team in participative goal-setting, have them help you assess the drivers of stress and increased resilience in your organization. Then make sure you walk the talk and model any commitments you are asking your people to make. Also think about how you can make your employees feel important and appreciated as you work through the process of cultural change.

◆ ◆ ◆

Chapter 24

Mindful Coaching

Coaching is best known in sports, where every top athlete has a coach. In the last twenty years coaching has also been adopted by organizations as a way of accelerating learning. Professional coaches are hired to help leaders develop in the context of a confidential relationship where they can let down their guard and experiment with new behaviors. HR, organizational and leadership development professionals are becoming trained in coaching skills so they can support executives' development. Leaders at all levels can learn coaching skills to build skills, engagement, and confidence in their employees. And mentors can use coaching skills to help high potential leaders develop skills, and navigate career choices.

Mindful coaching combines theory and research from modern coaching with the principles of focus and reflection. Mindful coaching is about helping clients focus their attention, learn new leadership skills, and make the MindShifts appropriate to their roles. Where reflection is private analysis, mindful coaching is reflecting in public. This reflection has the potential to transform how leaders work and how they define themselves.

At a macro level, mindful coaching is a continuous cycle of assessment (seeking understanding) and goal-setting (planning and action). The goal-setting phase helps clients see pragmatic value because it ensures progress toward concrete objectives. However, overfocusing on goals and outcomes can lead clients out of the moment and into frustration and tension where they do not learn. Rather than always checking and worrying about the score, clients need to pay attention to and enjoy the game (i.e., focus mindfully on their process).

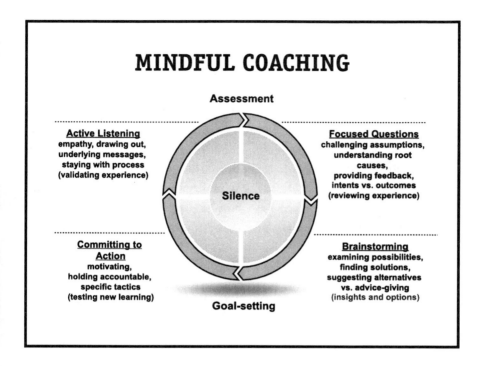

The coach creates a container of mindfulness, within which clients can think, feel, and experience without judgment, and which enables them to gradually reveal and accept themselves.[1] At the center of this container is **silence** — an underestimated source of knowing in itself and vital because freedom from interruption and peace of mind are essential for clear and productive thought. The coach also makes the intention to get out of the way by putting aside his or her own concerns in the interest of serving the client. This enables **active listening** where the coach goes beyond what is said to try to understand underlying themes. **Focused questions** direct the client's attention toward specific cues inside and around them. These questions shift perspective, challenge assumptions, and open the client up to new possibilities. In **brainstorming** the emphasis is on learning over teaching. The coach is active in providing new ideas, tools, models, and potential solutions. However, the coach is careful not to take over the client's choice by telling them what to do. The coach ensures results by asking the client to **commit to action** and execute a plan. The intention needs to come from the client for momentum to continue. The coach helps clients find the motivation to change and the courage to hold themselves accountable.

Mindful coaching facilitates the development of a broad range of leadership skills and related MindShifts. I find that coaching mindfully creates more sustained change than simply behavioral methods. One reason is that turning mindful attention to thoughts, feelings, and behavior helps undo self-destructive habits. In addition to raising awareness, giving ourselves and our clients accepting attention is healing in itself. As coaches, working mindfully helps us reflect on our own process and manage the ambiguity of our role. Not having ready-made answers and giving up control are anxiety producing and are central challenges for new coaches.[2]

My experience with Wendy, the executive who started her career as an administrative assistant, highlights the value of mindful coaching. Wendy's sanity, and my own, depended on my staying mindful during our meetings. When she interrupted herself mid-sentence to check her email, I was tempted to do the same. Instead, I monitored my frustration and observed her without judging. Reflecting back to her what I saw and asking questions about its impact helped her pay greater attention and look at herself with more clarity. Over time she began internalizing my accepting attention and started to cultivate greater mindfulness to contain her restless energy.

Experiment: Receiving Coaching

One of the best ways to learn to coach is to get a coach. A coach can help you take personal risks as well as learn to stay with and use feelings as a guide. Doing this helps you become more comfortable with your inner process and the experience of uncertainty, which are central to all types of learning. Look for someone who puts you at ease and who has had substantive training and experience. Make sure their coaching approach matches your goals and what you want to work on.

◆ ◆ ◆

Experiment: Providing Coaching

Once you have had the experience of being coached, offer to coach someone else. Coaching is a terrific way to develop mindfulness. Being mindful and centered is critical in order to track and use your emotional experience while coaching.

- Start by listening actively to your clients in order to understand their experience. Notice impulses to interrupt and reflect on what drives them.

- Notice any tendency to tell your clients what to do. Think about whether giving advice makes you feel more competent.

- Try to brainstorm ideas with your clients in a way that allows you to introduce options without taking over.

- Notice if you feel any impatience to have your clients take action or commit to change. We can often see the benefits of change more clearly than our clients. In order to manage our frustration we need to help our clients objectively assess their readiness to change. This can happen only when we set aside our own needs and desire for them to change.

◆ ◆ ◆

It is impossible and unwise to completely avoid giving advice in coaching. If a client is about to make their first boardroom presentation and is not prepared, the imperative is to ensure they do not make a fool of themselves. Ideally, though, the coach does not lead the client by the hand or provide specific directions. The coach's role is a learning facilitator rather than didactic teacher. This keeps responsibility with the clients and ensures they author their own experience.

Giving advice puts us into "expert" mode. The posture of all-knowing advisor feels good, but it can also be a defense against anxiety. We naturally have doubts about our own and our clients' capabilities. Seeing the world in black and white terms with us as the keepers of truth helps us feel secure. Unfortunately, after receiving advice clients often feel worse about themselves. They often feel "less-than" and incompetent for not having been able to get to answers on their own.

> People love to be told what to do, but they love even
> more to fight and not do what they are told. And thus
> they get entangled in hating the one who told them in
> the first place.   — *Carlos Castaneda*

When I reflect on coaching sessions, I sometimes notice preachy statements that I could more usefully have posed as questions. Questions invite clients to look and think rather than imposing our reality. Questions that come from genuine curiosity and interest also avoid the interpersonal push and condescension of advice. If I think a client is going in a risky direction I can usually make my point by asking about potential concerns and consequences rather than asserting conclusions.

Experiment: Increasing the Power of Questions

In your next coaching session, pay attention to your questions.

- Your value system influences what you attend to and the questions you ask. Think about what values are behind your questions.

- Notice how your questions focus your client's attention. Guiding your clients on how to allocate their attention may be the most important thing you do as a coach.

- Notice the impact of your questions on the quality of your client's reflection. Powerful questions provoke inquiry and greater mindfulness by opening up possibilities. They point out what could be rather than what is.

◆ ◆ ◆

Coaching is challenging because it presents a number of paradoxes. We want to help clients change, but to facilitate this we must accept them as they are. Only then can we help clients accept themselves. We naturally ally ourselves with the part of our clients that wants to change, but we need to be careful not to set up a battle with the part of them that wants to stay the same. We escape this paradox by cultivating our objectivity and neutrality. These qualities enable us to accept clients while believing in who they can become.

A pure coach role is hard because we often have a vested interest. Our client may be a friend or colleague whose behavior impacts us. This is one reason it is hard for managers to coach. Managers are paid for directing activities and getting things done, and so they may struggle with being nondirective and patient with change. It can help managers if they set aside dedicated coaching time so they can clearly separate managing from coaching. Over time managers start to see and trust in the value of coaching as a distinct activity.

Another balancing act coaches face is supporting clients while also challenging them. We begin coaching by establishing a strong working relationship, empathizing and joining with our clients' goals. In combination with positive feedback and encouragement this provides the foundation clients need to take risks. However, clients also need constructive feedback and life experiences that are frustrating and challenging. If we are too supportive, clients do not grow. If we are too challenging, they shut down.

Coaches are not expert consultants, and so they do not need to be more knowledgeable than their clients about their business. But they do need to have done the inner work they are asking their clients to do. We cannot model openness to learning and using feelings as a tool unless we have worked on ourselves. We cannot expect to transform our clients unless we have worked to transform ourselves. This is why ongoing supervision is so important for coaches. While transformation involves the most lasting change, there is a lot of important coaching work that is not transformational. A coach can also function as a sounding board and skills trainer, depending on how vulnerable the client is ready to be.

Using myself as a sounding board requires that my clients report events as accurately as possible. I then listen deeply and ask focused questions to raise awareness of behaviors, thoughts, feelings, and impacts. Being only a sounding board can be frustrating for coaches, but it is important not to underestimate the power of being heard and understood. This can be especially true for senior clients. Many CEOs have no one they can trust. Everyone around them is flattering them or borrowing their power. CEOs can also be more focused on navigating the political dance with their board, shareholders, and employees than in developing their skills or transforming themselves as leaders. Thus having a sounding board makes a lot of sense for them.

When clients can acknowledge areas of weakness (perhaps surfaced through an initial 360 or leadership style assessment) I can function as a skills development trainer. This mode of coaching skirts the boundaries of coach as expert or teacher and makes use of behavioral approaches such as practice, feedback, and modeling. I offer clients new behaviors and skills, and help them experiment in ways that build their confidence. I show clients how to reflect on their behavior and on the effectiveness of different learning styles. I also model reflection by talking about what is going on in coaching sessions and point out recurring or problematic patterns they bring into the relationship with me.

Transformation occurs when clients objectively evaluate their core values and assumptions. When clients undo the bind of self-limiting assumptions and beliefs, they open up new possibilities for being, thought, and action. Clients can begin to reflect on their life's purpose, reshape their personal philosophy, and align their behavior with their long-range goals. Insights from this work are potentially life-changing, as they enable clients to create meaning in new ways and redefine who they are.

Chapter 25

Who Are You?

"You are your attention," said the Guru.

"No I'm not," said Tom. "I'm here. I'm this body, these are my arms and legs and head."

"That's your body, parts of your body, but not You. You are not your body. That shirt you're wearing is yours, your shirt, but it is not You. You are not your shirt, or your pants, or your nose, or your piss. Or your girlfriend. They may be yours, but they are not You."

"So, who am I, then, or What am I?" asked Tom.

"I just told you. You are your attention. You are not the person who looks or feels or thinks, or wishes, or tells himself he wants, whatever he tells himself he wants."

"This all sounds like a lot of crap and double-talk. If I want something, who is wanting it if not me?"

"That depends on what you want, or need. If you want something that You really need, it may be really You who wants it. But if it's just something that your body wants, or thinks it wants, or your imagination thinks it needs, then it's not You, just your body or your imagination."

— Paul Ehrlich

Consciousness is made of attention and intention.[1] Attention produces growth and development wherever you focus it. Intention transforms that energy into information.

Attention is your flashlight. Wherever you point it you see more clearly. The flashlight is also healing. **When you attend nonjudgmentally to yourself or someone else, it is energizing without your adding any intention.** Tuning in to your body's signals in this way allows you to be

195

your own physician. You feel what is needed, and by paying attention you start to heal yourself.

Illness can be thought of as a call for attention and mindfulness. However, your body is not a mechanical object simply to fix when it breaks down. When you trust your body's symptoms and signals, your body responds with insight. The wisdom you gain by listening and feeling helps you unravel chance events, strange dreams, and complex life problems. In this way your body is a powerful ally and vital part of your consciousness.

Meditation can be thought of as self-focused attention with empathy. It is attention to yourself and your body with an attitude of acceptance. Meditation is inherently healing because it brings you closer to your true nature. It is focusing on your essence — attention, intention, joy, and happiness. Focusing the flashlight on the flashlight increases its intensity.

Experiment: Self-Inquiry Meditation

Self-inquiry meditation comes from the ancient tradition of Vedanta.[2] As in mindfulness meditation, you start by relaxing and creating an open, receptive quality in your attention. To this you add an active inquiry into the question "Who am I?" Rather than being an intellectual or conceptual question, this is a process of experiential discovery, using your body's felt sense as the pathway and anchor for your attention.

- Sit or lie down so you are comfortable.
- Take a minute to breathe and settle into your body.
- Slowly scan down through your body from head to toe, feeling closely into each area.
- Explore into each subtle sensation that comes up and into the contrast between how different areas feel.
- Rather than observing your body from your head, try to experience your body from inside your body.
- Scan through your body again from head to toe, noticing if your experience has shifted.
- Pay attention to the you who is observing, witnessing, and attending.

- Notice if the you who is watching and the you who is being watched merge. This is the experience of yourself beyond subject/object consciousness.

◆ ◆ ◆

Rory was head of the innovation lab for a consumer packaged goods company. His group was an incubator for new products, and he had personally patented several ideas that had significantly boosted his company's market share. His boss told me there was no one who was better at inventing the future than Rory. Unfortunately, Rory didn't care as much whether anyone else in the company saw the value in his ideas. He just liked creating them. In fact, he didn't seem to care much about people at all. The result was a large number of his ideas were left on the shelf.

I asked Rory where he got his ideas. He didn't know, so I asked him to observe his creative process. After a few weeks he told me his ideas just appeared. He had learned to put himself in a flow-like trance when he worked in the lab, and it was then that he received his best ideas. I asked Rory if he thought ideas came from his unconscious. He wasn't sure what an unconscious was. I had to admit it was hard to define.

Rory was from India and had grown up Hindu. He saw his self as a small part of a larger consciousness or Self. He was an active meditator and believed his ideas ultimately came from tapping into and trusting the creative intelligence of that true Self. He defined that Self as pure being, pure attention, and said it was the same thing I would call Spirit or God.

Rory rationalized that too much desire, too much attachment to a commercial outcome, would kill his creative process. He believed that when he worked or meditated he got in touch with a field of pure potential. He could add a little bit of intention to this field of open attention, and as long as it was not with attachment or desire, it would have an organizing effect. I could not disagree with him philosophically. However, practically, I felt there must be some way his company could get more use from his ideas.

I was impressed with Rory's intellect and ability to articulate an integrated spiritual perspective. Moreover, Rory had learned how to put his conscious, effortful will on hold, so he could allow ideas to come to him. I had taught many people to tap into this "soft will" using self-hypnosis, but he had learned to access it on his own. As I completed a leadership assessment and got feedback from his colleagues, though, I came to the conclusion that his emotional and interpersonal awareness was far less developed.

Rory acted as if people did not matter to him. He seldom made eye contact when he passed people in the hall and barely acknowledged colleagues when he participated in larger meetings. Senior executives dismissed him as a technician who had limited ability to follow through and therefore limited potential as a leader.

Rory was, in fact, quite sensitive to what people thought of him. He was prone to personalizing and could easily get attached to distorted perceptions and assumptions. I asked him to examine some of these reactions with the same attitude and openness he used in meditation. He gradually started to understand the unintended impact he was having with his behavior.

I next worked with Rory to bring greater attention to his intention. We focused on his core values and on prioritization and goal-setting. As he aligned his values with his actions, his leadership started to become more authentic. He actually did care a great deal about people and about the growth and development of his staff. He just had little idea how to help them, and so he gave them the same treatment he wanted — i.e., he left them alone.

Rory learned to listen and coach his people without solving their problems. In addition, he thought about his intention before trying to give staff feedback. He realized that he typically dreaded giving feedback, hoping only that the person "got the message." When he instead focused on how he could support the person's growth, it changed the tone of his conversations and the receptivity to his feedback.

Rory had a great deal of willpower, perseverance, and self-discipline. He had likely developed these aspects of concentrated intention over years of meditating. However, he had never chosen to apply these skills to relationships. He was introverted and self-reliant and had not thought about how to get work done through others. We turned his analytical mind toward win/win negotiating and relationship mapping. He reflected and clarified his intention before meetings with peers, and soon he was starting to build stronger relationships and greater momentum for his ideas across the organization.

Rory spent less time innovating in his lab. At the same time, the number of ideas he and his team implemented rose dramatically. Rory was initially surprised that he did not miss spending more time creating. He had learned to value a new set of activities that were actually more in line with his values of service, contribution, and the development of people.

Experiment: Experiencing Subtle Forms of Communication

What do you think is the quickest and most accurate form of communication? Most people would say spoken words. It turns out that facial expressions communicate feelings more clearly, and that touch is actually the most precise and powerful form of communication.[3]

You can experiment with communication beyond touch with a simple experiment:

+ Relax your body and take a few mindful breaths.

+ Ask a friend to hold their palm about an inch away from yours.

+ Focus on the sensations in your hand, continuing to hold your hand there for at least thirty seconds.

+ Expand your attention to include your stomach, midsection, and the rest of your body.

+ Notice whatever sensations come up.

+ Share what you felt with your partner.

◆ ◆ ◆

You were born thinking of yourself as the whole world. Then you experienced yourself as an extension of your mother. The process of learning you were a unique individual came with a great deal of anxiety. You could not meet most of your needs on your own and began to realize how vulnerable you were. You were socialized into the rules of your family, who taught you how to be "good" so you could stay connected to your sources of nurturance and care. This formed the core of your identity.

You added additional rules about who you are as you grew, many of which involved how to make sure others approved of you. This meant competing for attention. Attention felt good because it made you feel connected. You reinforced different aspects of yourself in your effort to sustain the identity you created. If you were unlucky, and got little positive attention for who you were, you may have developed a special sense of deficit. Now you may have a greater need to get attention to sustain yourself.

We take long trips.
We puzzle over the meaning of a painting or a book,
When what we are wanting to see and understand in this world,
We are that.   —*Rumi*

As an adult you get glimmers of experience that suggest the self you created is not really you. Your persona is a self-fulfilling dream. You expect to be a certain way, and others come to expect that behavior from you, and so sometimes you get stuck. You cling to one particular identity that stops fitting what is needed in the moment. But you persist and start to question these expectations and rules more objectively. How did you get attached to these goals? Are they really yours, or are you something else?

Practicing silence and solitude helps you break out of this identity and deconstruct it. You are able to clear away the clutter of history, roles, and expertise that has defined you. Accepting and exploring your experience in the present, you gradually build a more stable sense of self from the inside out. You realize how absurd it is when you meet someone who immediately asks, "So what do you do?" as if that will tell them who you are. It is only a story. **Who you are is not what you do.**

As you strengthen your attention, you realize that you are not your thoughts. Awareness exists in you independently. Continuing to focus on awareness you realize thoughts and feelings change constantly, as does everything in the world around you. You become more comfortable with impermanence. Detaching from your thinking and approval-seeking gives you a greater sense of stability and peace. You become less afraid and start to see reality more clearly. You recognize that your self is a construction and your personality is a fiction. You become whatever you dream.

Your final task is relearning that you are in fact not alone, that loneliness is a fantasy. You are inextricably linked to everything and everyone around you. Your larger Self includes everything.

Strawberries are too delicate to be picked by machine. The perfectly ripe ones bruise at even too heavy a human touch. It hit her then that every strawberry she had ever eaten — every piece of fruit — had been picked by callused human hands. Every piece of toast with jelly represented someone's knees, someone's aching back and hips, someone with a bandana on her wrist to wipe away the sweat. Why had no one told her about this before?   —*Alison Luterman*

As you widen your focus, you broaden your identity beyond your isolated ego. This frees you from a mean, survival-based mentality. This enables you to determine what your real needs are, not just what your body or imagination thinks it needs. Thinking more holistically about yourself you are also able to cooperate and work flexibly in the complex organizational and global system in which you live. Broadening your self-definition enables you to develop socially conscious leadership. The more you see, the more you appreciate your impact on your community and the planet.

This can be a tough world. At times just surviving seems hard enough. You can make life more joyful and fulfilling when you realize who you are. Then your challenge is finding ways to remember this truth. When you lose touch with your essence, life quickly becomes an unending series of miserable tasks. When you forget yourself and your attention, you lose your ability to stop, reflect, and focus. When you come back to yourself, you are able to consciously attend and intend. In addition, you reawaken the wonder and playfulness you were born with. This openness enables you to learn essential leadership skills and avoid common habit traps. This does not mean an end to pain or fear or sadness. Staying connected to who you are, you can ride the waves of feeling and experience more skillfully and get where you want more purposefully and effectively.

Acknowledgments

I am indebted to so many people.

My wife, Lisa, supported me and put up with countless hours of me hunched over the computer while I worked on how to articulate these ideas. My daughter, Taylor, would rather have played with me but showed great understanding, especially for a two year old. My mother-in-law, Bear-Bear Ireland, took care of Taylor on many weekends, allowing me time to write.

My parents, Paul and Isabelle, brother, Julian, and father-in-law, David, all took an active interest and supported me. It was at a family reunion at David's house in Austin that I wrote the first article that formed the core of the book. My brother-in-law, Larry, his wife, Tami, and David's wife, Diane, all read the article and helped me shape the direction of the book.

My clients shared themselves with me and taught me about leadership and their businesses. Their inspiring lives and stories are the heart of this book. Many offered quotes that further brought the ideas to life.

The 2009 financial crisis and subsequent recession gave me a gift — time to reflect, focus, and crystallize my thoughts. As I reflected I realized that my coaching centered around the management of attention and that my clients were learning to lead by focusing their attention on specific cues in themselves and others.

Dr. Alan Ajaya was the first to teach me about attention, self-inquiry, and self-acceptance. Gregor Simon-MacDonald taught me the meaning of the "I am," and as a deep thinker, seeker, and ally, he provided early feedback that was pivotal in getting me out of my head as I wrote. Karen Muchnick was always there for me and gave me many ideas on how to make the writing clearer. Marty Livingston was an important mentor who taught me about staying with the process.

Howard Smagula and Robert Gartman were true friends who believed in me and gave me the encouragement I needed to continue. Close readings by Mark Hurwich and Susan Toback came just at the right time, when my eyes were glazed over from looking at the same words too many times. Bill O'Connor provided incredible precision with his edits and eye for detail.

My guiding light through the publishing process was Mike O'Malley. It takes a courageous man to write an incisive book like *Leading with Kindness*. It takes an even more impressive human being to live kindness so completely. Mike stuck with me through many challenging periods and was unwavering in his support and belief in me. For that I will always be grateful.

Thank you all.

Notes

Chapter 1 / The Challenge

1. Edward Hallowell, *Crazy Busy* (New York: Ballantine Books, 2006). Stephan Rechtschaffen, *Time Shifting* (London: Rider, 1997).

2. Matt Richtel, "Attached to Technology and Paying a Price," *New York Times*, June 6, 2010, New York ed.

3. S. Brave and C. Nass, "Emotion in Human-Computer Interaction," in *The Human-Computer Interaction Handbook*, ed. J. Jacko and A. Sears (Mahwah, N.J.: Lawrence Erlbaum Associates, 2003), 81–93).

4. Basex, Inc. (2010). *http://en.wikipedia.org/wiki/Basex*.

5. Jon Hamilton, "Think You're Multitasking? Think Again," National Public Radio, October 2, 2008.

6. Robert B. Kaiser, Robert Hogan, and S. Bartholomew Craig, "Leadership and the Fate of Organizations," *American Psychologist* (2008) *doi:* 10.1037/0003-066X.63.2.96.

7. Norman F. Dixon, *On the Psychology of Military Incompetence* (New York: Basic Books, 1976).

8. H. L. Tosi, V. F. Misangyi, A. Fanelli, D. A. Waldman, and F. J. Yammarino, "CEO Charisma, Compensation, and Firm Performance," *Leadership Quarterly* 15 (2004): 405–20. B. R. Agle, N. J. Nagarajan, J. A. Sonnenfeld, and D. Srinivasan, "Does CEO Charisma Matter? An Empirical Analysis of the Relationships among Organizational Performance, Environmental Uncertainty, and Top Management Team Perception of CEO Charisma," *Academy of Management Journal* 49 (2006): 161–74.

9. Robert Goffee and Gareth Jones, *Why Should Anyone Be Led by You* (Boston: Harvard Business School Press, 2006).

10. Daniel Goleman, "Leadership That Gets Results," *Harvard Business Review* 78 (2000): 78–90.

11. Bill George and Peter Sims, *True North* (San Francisco: Jossey-Bass, 2007).

12. J. Collins, "Level 5 Leadership: The Triumph of Humility and Fierce Resolve," *Harvard Business Review* 79, no. 1 (2001b): 66–76.

13. William F. Baker and Michael O'Malley, *Leading with Kindness* (New York: AMACOM, 2008).

14. Robert Schaffer "Demand Better Results — and Get Them," *Harvard Business Review* (March–April 1991).

Part I: Three Core Disciplines

1. Gordon Spence, *New Directions in Evidence-Based Coaching* (Saarbrücken: VDM Verlag Dr. Müller, 2008).
2. Daniel Goleman, "Finding Happiness: Cajole Your Brain to Lean to the Left," *New York Times,* February 4, 2003, sec. F: 5.
3. R. G. Baumeister and T. F. Heatherton, "Self-regulation Failure: An Overview," *Psychological Inquiry* 7, no. 1 (1996): 1–15.
4. J. Kabat-Zinn, *Full Catastrophe Living* (New York: Bantam Doubleday Dell, 1990). B. Alan Wallace and Shauna L. Shapiro, "Mental Balance and Well-Being: Building Bridges between Buddhism and Western Psychology," *American Psychologist* 61 (2006): 690–701.
5. Ellen J. Langer, *The Power of Mindful Learning* (New York: Da Capo Press, 1998).
6. Franklin Stein, "Occupational Stress, Relaxation Therapies, Exercise and Biofeedback," *Work: A Journal of Prevention, Assessment and Rehabilitation* 17, no. 3 (2001): 235–45.

Chapter 2 / Stopping

1. Shamsi Iqbal and Eric Horvitz, "Disruption and Recovery of Computing Tasks: Field Study, Analysis, and Directions," *CHI* (April 28–May 3, 2007).
2. Sharon Melnick, "Personal Productivity Strategies for Dealing with Distractions, Politics, and Work Overload," ASTD New York, September 15, 2010.
3. European Industrial Relations Observatory (2009), "Working Time Developments." *www.eurofound.europa.eu/eiro/studies/tn1004039s/tn1004039s.htm.*
4. Families and Work Institute (2004),"Overwork in America: When the Way We Work Becomes Too Much." *http://familiesandwork.org/site/research/summary/overwork2005summ.pdf.*
5. Jennifer Anderson, "Report Highlights Gap between European and U.S. Vacation Time," Ergoweb, May 15, 2005. *www.ergoweb.com/news/detail.cfm?id=1106.*
6. James Maas, *Power Sleep* (New York: HarperCollins, 2001).
7. "To Sleep, Perchance to Dream..."*Oxford Health Care Healthy Mind Healthy Body* (Summer 1998): 11.
8. Alice Kuhn Schwartz and Norma S. Aaron, *Somniquest: The 5 Types of Sleeplessness and How to Overcome Them* (New York: Harmony Books, 1979).

Chapter 3 / Reflecting

1. Justin Menkes, *Executive Intelligence: What All Great Leaders Have* (New York: HarperCollins, 2005).
2. Bruch Heike and Jochen I. Menges, "The Acceleration Trap," *Harvard Business Review* (April 2010). Jim Collins, *Good to Great: Why Some Companies Make the Leap...and Others Don't* (New York: Harper Business, 2001).
3. Heike and Menges, "The Acceleration Trap."

4. C. Argyris, *Overcoming Organizational Defenses — Facilitating Organizational Learning* (Boston: Allyn and Bacon, 1990).

5. R. Shaw and D. Perkins, "Teaching Organizations to Learn: The Power of Productive Failures," in D. Nadler, M. Gerstein, and R. Shaw, *Organizational Architecture: Designs for Changing Organizations* (San Francisco: Jossey-Bass, 1992).

6. Department of the Army, *The Leader's Guide to After-Action Reviews* (1993). *www.au.af.mil/au/awc/awcgate/army/tc_25-20/tc25-20.pdf.*

Chapter 4 / Learning through Reflecting

1. Michael M. Lombardo and Robert W. Eichinger, *The Leadership Machine: Architecture to Develop Leaders for Any Future* (Boston: Lominger International, 2000).

2. Peter Honey and Alan Mumford, *The Learning Styles Questionnaire* (Maidenhead, Berkshire: Peter Honey Publications, 2000). David A. Kolb, *The Kolb Learning Style Inventory* (Philadelphia: Hay Group, 1999).

3. George K. Kriflik, Ph.D., and Lynda Kriflik, Ph.D., "Leadership Learning: Building on Grounded Theory to Explore the Role of Critical Reflection in Leadership Learning," University of Wollongong, 20th ANZAM Conference, December 2006, Australia.

4. Kathy Doncaster, *Reflection Handbook for the Master's in Professional Development*, Professional Development Foundation and National Center for Work-based Partnerships (London: Middlesex University, 1999).

5. Donald A. Schon, *Educating the Reflective Practitioner* (San Francisco: Jossey-Bass, 1987).

6. David E. Gray, "Facilitating Management Learning: Developing Critical Reflection through Reflective Tools," *Sage Journals Online* (2008).

7. Mary L. Burton and Richard A. Wedemeyer, *In Transition* (New York: Collins, 1992).

Chapter 5 / Focusing

1. Thich Nhat Hanh, *Peace Is Every Step* (New York: Bantam, 1992).

2. Tara Brach, *Radical Acceptance: Embracing Your Life with the Heart of a Buddha* (New York: Bantam, 2004).

Chapter 6 / Learning through Focusing

1. Michael M. Lombardo and Robert W. Eichinger, *The Leadership Machine: Architecture to Develop Leaders for Any Future* (Boston: Lominger International, 2000).

2. J. Ehrlich, N. M. Boulis, T. Karrer, C. L. Sahley, "Differential Effects of Serotonin Depletion on Sensitization and Dishabituation in the Leech," *Journal of Neurobiology* 23 (1992): 270–79.

3. Pema Chodron, *Getting Unstuck: Breaking Your Habitual Patterns and Encountering Naked Reality* (Solon, Oh.: Playaway, 2009).

4. Ellen J. Langer, *The Power of Mindful Learning* (New York: Da Capo Press, 1998).

5. Jon Kabat-Zinn, *Coming to Our Senses: Healing Ourselves and the World through Mindfulness* (New York: Hyperion, 2005).

6. Sidney Rosen and Milton H. Erickson, *My Voice Will Go with You: The Teaching Tales of Milton H. Erickson* (Boston: W. W. Norton, 1991).

7. Ernest Lawrence Rossi, *Psychobiology of Mind-Body Healing: New Concepts of Therapeutic Hypnosis* (New York: W. W. Norton, 1993).

8. Arnold Mindell, *The Shaman's Body: A New Shamanism for Transforming Health, Relationships, and Community* (San Francisco: HarperSanFrancisco, 1993).

9. M. W. McCall, M. M. Lombardo, and A. M. Morrison, *The Lessons of Experience* (New York: Free Press, 1988).

10. Carey Bongard, "What Is the Assurant Executive Profile?" master's thesis in professional development (executive coaching) (London: Middlesex University, 2008).

Chapter 7 / MindShifting

1. R. Charan, S. Drotter, and J. Noel, *The Leadership Pipeline: How to Build the Leadership-powered Company* (San Francisco: Jossey-Bass, 2001).

Chapter 8 / Values and Purpose

1. Bill George and Peter Sims, *True North* (San Francisco: Jossey-Bass, 2007).

2. K. M. Sheldon and A. J. Elliot, " Goal Striving, Need Satisfaction, and Longitudinal Well-Being: The Self-Concordance Model," *Journal of Personality and Social Psychology* 76, no. 3 (1999): 482–97.

3. "Connecting Organizational Communication to Financial Performance — 2003/2004 Communication ROI Study," Watson Wyatt Worldwide (2004).

4. Jonathan Golub, personal communication, 2008.

5. Hewitt Associates, "Can You Overcome the Talent Crisis?" New York, October 14, 1998.

6. Sam Mamudi, "Socially Responsible Funds Reap Rewards in Uncharitable Market," *Wall Street Journal, MarketWatch,* November 2, 2008.

Chapter 9 / Strategic Thinking

1. Warren Bennis, *Why Leaders Can't Lead: The Unconscious Conspiracy Continues* (San Francisco: Jossey-Bass, 1997).

Chapter 10 / Innovative Thinking

1. Dow Kim, "Innovation in Global Markets," The 2007 Merrill Lynch Global Innovation Program, New York, April 18, 2007.

2. Barry Nalebuff and Ian Ayers, *Why Not? How to Use Everyday Ingenuity to Solve Problems Big and Small* (Cambridge, Mass.: Harvard Business School Press.

3. Edward Hallowell, *Crazy Busy* (New York: Ballantine, 2006).

4. Roderick Gilkey and Clint Kilts, "Cognitive Fitness," *Harvard Business Review* 85 (2007): 53–66.

5. H. G. Gough, "A Creative Personality Scale for the Adjective Check List," *Journal of Personality and Social Psychology* 37 (1979): 1398–1405.

6. Nancy Kline, *Time to Think* (London: Ward Lock Publishing, 1999).

7. Teresa M. Amabile, *Keys: Assessing the Climate for Creativity* (Greensboro, N.C.: Center for Creative Leadership, 1995).

8. Jim Andrew, "Payback: Reaping the Rewards of Innovation," The 2007 Merrill Lynch Global Innovation Program, New York, April 18, 2007.

9. Chip Heath and Dan Heath, *Made to Stick: Why Some Ideas Survive and Others Die* (New York: Random House, 2007).

10. Jim Loehr and Tony Schwartz, "The Making of a Corporate Athlete," *Harvard Business Review* 79 (2001): 118–28. Daniel Goleman and Richard Boyatzis, "Social Intelligence and the Biology of Leadership," *Harvard Business Review* 86 (2008): 74–81.

Chapter 11 / Stress Management and Resilience

1. Roderick Gilkey and Clint Kilts, "Cognitive Fitness," *Harvard Business Review* 85 (2007): 53–66.

2. Sadie F. Dingfelder, "An Insidious Enemy," *Monitor on Psychology* (October 2008): 20–24.

3. Brenda J. Thames, EdD, ed. "Stress Management for the Health of It," *NASD*, February 1997. Clemson University. September 29, 2008. *www.cdc.gov/nasd/docs/ d001201-d001300/d001245/d001245.pdf.*

4. J. Kabat-Zinn, *Full Catastrophe Living* (New York: Bantam Doubleday Dell, 1990). Tony Schwartz and Catherine McCarthy, "Manage Your Energy, Not Your Time," *Harvard Business Review* 85 (2007). Sara Martin, "The Power of the Relaxation Response," *Monitor on Psychology* (October 2008): 30–34.

5. Daniel Goleman and Richard Boyatzis, "Social Intelligence and the Biology of Leadership," *Harvard Business Review* 86 (2008): 74–81.

6. Laurence Gonzales, *Deep Survival: Who Lives, Who Dies, and Why* (Boston: W. W. Norton, 2003).

7. Marianne Frankenhaeuser, "The Psychophysiology of Workload, Stress and Health: Comparison between the Sexes. Mine-series: Behavioral Medicine: An Interpersonal Perspective," *Annals of Behavioral Medicine* 13, no. 4 (1990): 197–204.

8. Matthieu Ricard, "Change Your Mind Change Your Brain: The Inner Conditions for Authentic Happiness," Google Tech Talks. Google Headquarters, 1600 Amphitheatre Parkway, Mountain View, Calif., March 15, 2007.

9. Jim Loehr and Tony Schwartz. "The Making of a Corporate Athlete," *Harvard Business Review* 79 (2001): 118–28.

10. Epictetus, *The Enchiridion Epictetus*, trans. Thomas W. Higginson (Indianapolis: Bobbs-Merrill, 1955).

11. Joshua Ehrlich, "Vulnerability to Depressive Affect Following Failure: The Role of Personality and Cognition" (doctoral dissertation, New York University, 1996).

12. Aaron T. Beck, *Cognitive Therapy and the Emotional Disorders* (New York: Meridian Book, 1979).

13. Bill George and Peter Sims, *True North* (San Francisco: Jossey-Bass, 2007).

Chapter 12 / Communication

1. Thich Nhat Hanh, "Mindfulness in Everyday Life," Omega Institute, Rhinebeck, N.Y., August 2, 1998.

2. "Emory Study Lights Up the Political Brain," *Science Daily,* January 31, 2006.

3. Gregor Simon-MacDonald, lectures on Mindfulness, Anthroposophical Society of New York, 2000.

4. Howard J. Markman, *Working with High-Conflict Couples,* Center for Marital and Family Studies, Family Therapy Network Symposium, March 24, 1995, University of Denver.

5. John Groom, 2008. Personal communication — mindful listening warm up exercise.

6. Bill George and Peter Sims, *True North* (San Francisco: Jossey-Bass, 2007).

Chapter 13 / Emotional Intelligence

1. P. Salovey and J. D. Mayer, "Emotional Intelligence," *Imagination, Cognition, and Personality* 9 (1990): 185–211.

2. Lyle Spencer, "The Emotionally Intelligent Workplace: How to Select For, Measure, and Improve Emotional Intelligence," in *Individuals, Groups, and Organizations* (San Francisco: Jossey-Bass, 2001), chapter 4. J. D. Mayer, P. Salovey, and D. R. Caruso, "Emotional Intelligence: New Ability or Eclectic Traits?" *American Psychologist* 63, no. 6 (2008): 503–17.

3. Ibid.

4. Jeremy D. Safran, Ph.D., J. Christopher Muran, Ph.D., and Elizabeth Muran, Ph.D., "Emotion in Psychotherapy," presented to the Cognitive-Interpersonal Therapy Group, April 23, 1994, Williams Club, New York.

5. Thich Nhat Hanh, "Mindfulness in Everyday Life." Omega Institute, Rhinebeck, N.Y., August 2, 1998. Matthieu Ricard, "Change Your Mind Change Your Brain: The Inner Conditions for Authentic Happiness," Google Tech Talks, Google Headquarters, 1600 Amphitheatre Parkway, Mountain View, Calif., March 15, 2007.

6. Swami Ajaya, *Healing the Whole Person* (New York: Himalayan Institute Press, 2008).

7. Paul Eckman, "SIOP 2008 Invited Address: Emotional Skills," *The Industrial-Organizational Psychologist* 46 (2008): 21–24.

8. Candance B. Pert and Deepak Chopra, *Molecules of Emotion : The Science behind Mind-Body Medicine* (New York: Scribner, 1999).

9. Jon Kabat-Zinn, "The Science of Mindfulness," *Speaking of Faith,* National Public Radio, April 18, 2009.

10. Jon Kabat-Zinn, *Full Catastrophe Living* (New York: Bantam Doubleday Dell, 1990). Tony Schwartz and Catherine McCarthy. "Manage Your Energy, Not Your Time," *Harvard Business Review* 85 (2007).

11. Daniel Goleman, "Finding Happiness: Cajole Your Brain to Lean to the Left," *New York Times* February 4, 2003, sec. F: 5.

12. Matthieu, "Change Your Mind Change Your Brain." S. L. Shapiro, G. E. Schwartz, and G. Bonner, "Effects of Mindfulness-Based Stress Reduction on Medical and Premedical Students," *Journal of Behavioral Medicine* 21, no. 6 (1998): 581–99.

13. R. F. Baumeister and T. F. Heatherton, "Self-regulation Failure: An Overview," *Psychological Inquiry* 7, no. 1 (1996): 1–15. Alan B. Wallace and Shauna L. Shapiro, "Mental Balance and Well-Being: Building Bridges between Buddhism and Western Psychology," *American Psychologist* 61 (2006): 690–701.

14. Roderick Gilkey and Clint Kilts, "Cognitive Fitness," *Harvard Business Review* 85 (2007): 53–66.

Chapter 14 / Relationship Building, Negotiating, and Networking

1. Thich Nhat Hanh, *Teachings on Love* (Berkeley, Calif.: Parallax Press, 2006).

2. Bob Wall, *Working Relationships: The Simple Truth about Getting Along with Friends and Foes at Work* (Grand Rapids, Mich.: Davies-Black, 1999).

3. John P. Kotter, *John P. Kotter on What Leaders Really Do* (New York: Harvard Business School Press, 1999).

Chapter 15 / Leading and Developing Teams

1. Edgar H. Schein, *Process Consultation,* vol. 1: *Its Role in Organization Development* (New York: Addison-Wesley Longman, 1988).

2. Victor H. Vroom and Philip W. Yetton, *Leadership and Decision-Making* (Pittsburgh: University of Pittsburgh Press, 1976).

3. Joseph E. McCann and Thomas N. Gilmore, "Diagnosing Organizational Decision Making through Responsibility Charting," *Sloan Management Review* (Winter 1983): 3.

4. Larry Hirschhorn and Thomas Gilmore, "The New Boundaries of the 'Boundaryless' Company," *Harvard Business Review* 70 (1992): 104–15.

5. Schein, *Process Consultation.*

Chapter 16 / Habits

1. Alex Stajkovic, "Subconscious Priming and Goal-setting," SIOP, New Orleans, April 3, 2009.

2. Thomas M. Sterner, *The Practicing Mind: Bringing Discipline and Focus into Your Life* (Wilmington, Del.: Mountain Sage, 2006).

3. Dan Leighton Taigen, *Cultivating the Empty Field: The Silent Illumination of Zen Master Hongzhi* (Boston: Tuttle Publishing, 2000).

4. Stephan Rechtschaffen, *Time Shifting* (London: Rider, 1997).

5. Sterner, *The Practicing Mind.*

6. John Bradshaw, *Healing the Shame That Binds You* (Deerfield Beach, Fla.: Health Communications, 2005).

7. Pema Chodron, *Getting Unstuck* (Boulder, Colo.: Sounds True, 2009).

Chapter 17 / Perfectionism, Self-Criticism, and Self-Confidence

1. Pema Chodron, *Getting Unstuck* (Boulder, Colo.: Sounds True, 2009).

2. Joshua Ehrlich, "Dysfunctional Attitudes, Emotional Responses, and Physiological Correlates of Induced-Failure Stress" (M.A. thesis, New York University, 1994).

3. Joshua Ehrlich, "Vulnerability to Depressive Affect Following Failure: The Role of Personality and Cognition" (doctoral dissertation, New York University, 1996).

4. J. A. Colquitt, J. A. LePine, and R. A. Noe, "Toward an Integrative Theory of Training and Motivation: A Meta-Analytic Path Analysis of 20 Years of Research," *Journal of Applied Psychology* 85, no. 5 (2000): 678–707.

5. Ellen J. Langer, *The Power of Mindful Learning* (New York: Da Capo Press, 1998).

6. Bill George and Peter Sims, *True North* (San Francisco: Jossey-Bass, 2007).

7. Mark Hurwich, personal communication, 2010.

8. Mihaly Csikszentmihalyi, *Flow: The Psychology of Optimal Experience* (New York: Harper and Row, 1990).

9. Swami Ajaya, *Healing the Whole Person* (New York: Himalayan Institute Press, 2008).

10. Tara Brach, *Radical Acceptance: Embracing Your Life with the Heart of a Buddha* (New York: Bantam, 2004).

11. Gordon Spence, *New Directions in Evidence-Based Coaching* (Saarbrücken: VDM Verlag Dr. Mueller e.K., 2008).

Chapter 18 / Negative and Irrational Thinking

1. Rebecca Leung, "Sea Gypsies See Signs in the Waves," *60 Minutes*, CBS News, August 21, 2005. November 10, 2009. *www.cbsnews.com/stories/2005/08/17/60minutes/main782658.shtml?source=search_story.*

2. Maggie Jackson, *Distracted: The Erosion of Attention and the Coming Dark Age* (New York: Prometheus Books, 2008).

3. David G. Myers, *Psychology*, 9th ed. (New York: Worth, 2010).

4. Deepak Chopra, *Seven Spiritual Laws of Success: A Practical Guide to the Fulfillment of Your Dreams* (San Rafael, Calif.: Amber-Allen, New World Library, 1994).

5. A. D. Ong, C. S. Bergeman, T. L. Bisconti, and K. A. Wallace, "Psychological Resilience, Positive Emotions, and Successful Adaptation to Stress in Later Life," *Journal of Personality and Social Psychology* 91 (2006): 730–49.

6. David Cooperrider and Diana Whitney, *Appreciative Inquiry: A Positive Revolution in Change* (San Francisco: Berrett-Koehler, 2005).

7. Janice Fleming, "What Traits Predict Coachability?" thesis (London: Middlesex University–Institute for Work-Based Learning, 2009).

Chapter 19 / Tolerating Uncertainty and Change

1. Thich Nhat Hanh, "Mindfulness in Everyday Life," Omega Institute, Rhinebeck, N.Y., August 2, 1998. Thomas M. Sterner, *The Practicing Mind: Bringing Discipline and Focus into Your Life* (Wilmington, Del.: Mountain Sage, 2006).

2. Ethan Schutz, "Wants, Not Needs: A Key Part of the Evolution of FIRO Theory," Schutz Company, 2009.

3. Elisabeth Kübler-Ross and David Kessler, *On Grief and Grieving: Finding the Meaning of Grief through the Five Stages of Loss* (New York: Scribner, 2007).

Chapter 20 / Multitasking and Technology

1. S. W. Lazar et al., "Meditation Experiences Is Associated with Increase Cortical Thickness," *Neuroreport* 16, no. 17 (2005): 1893–97.

2. Matt Richtel, "Lost in Email, Tech Firms Face Self-Made Beast," *New York Times,* June 14, 2008, Technology sec. See also Larry D. Rosen, "Help! I'm Drowning in Information," *National Psychologist* 13 (2004).

3. Ellen J. Langer, *The Power of Mindful Learning* (New York: Da Capo Press, 1998).

Chapter 21 / Prioritization and Time Management

1. Stephen Hawking, *A Brief History of Time* (New York: Bantam, 1998).

2. Stephen Covey, *The Seven Habits of Highly Effective People* (New York: Free Press, 1990).

Chapter 22 / Goal Setting and Development Planning

1. Daniel Goleman, "Leadership That Gets Results," *Harvard Business Review* 78 (2000): 78–90.

2. Peter Drucker, *The Practice of Management,* 2nd ed. (New York: HarperCollins, 2007).

3. E. A. Locke and G. P. Latham, "Building a Practically Useful Theory of Goal Setting and Task Motivation," *American Psychologist* 57 (2002): 705–17.

4. Jack Mezirow, *Fostering Critical Reflection in Adulthood: A Guide to Transformative and Emancipatory Learning* (San Francisco: Jossey-Bass, 1990).

Chapter 23 / Organizational Goals and Focus

1. Warren Bennis, *Why Leaders Can't Lead: The Unconscious Conspiracy Continues* (San Francisco: Jossey-Bass, 1997).

Chapter 24 / Mindful Coaching

1. D. W. Winnicott, *Playing and Reality* (New York: Routledge Classics, 2005).

2. David Hosmer, "Cascading Coaching: Building a Model of Peer Development," *OD Practitioner* 38, no. 3 (2006): 17–20.

Chapter 25 / Who Are You?

1. Deepak Chopra, *Seven Spiritual Laws of Success: A Practical Guide to the Fulfillment of Your Dreams* (San Rafael, Calif.: Amber-Allen, New World Library, 1994).

2. Allan Ajaya, personal communication: self-inquiry meditation, 2005.

3. Amy Novotney, "The Evolution of Human Goodness," *Monitor on Psychology* 40, no. 5 (2009): 24–26.

Index of Experiments

JOSHUA EHRLICH is an organizational consultant, executive coach, and a supervisor and accreditor of coaches. He advises CEOs and facilitates top teams to achieve complex business objectives. Josh has provided coaching and talent management consulting to hundreds of senior executives in multinational companies. His clients include more than fifty of the Fortune 100 across diverse industries..

In 2010 he founded the Global Leadership Council — an international network of experts in leadership and organizational transformation. Josh provides advanced training for leaders and OD/LD professionals in coaching and mentoring, and serves as a Master Coach Supervisor for the European Coaching and Mentoring Council. He speaks to a variety of audiences about certification standards and brings together coaches from around the world to teach best practices. He has contributed to the *Harvard Business Review,* the *Wall Street Journal,* and NPR.

Josh is a leading authority on succeeding in demanding environments. His research at Yale and New York University and numerous articles have clarified the psychological and physiological mechanisms by which stress impairs effectiveness. Based on his findings, he helps individuals, teams, and organizations to develop their resilience through mindfulness training.

For more about Dr. Ehrlich see *www.globalleadershipcouncil.com*

CPSIA information can be obtained at www.ICGtesting.com
Printed in the USA
BVOW01s1123070314

346952BV00002B/3/P